Penguin
LIVES

HERMAN MELVILLE

A LIPPER / VIKING BOOK

GENERAL EDITOR: JAMES ATLAS

ELIZABETH HARDWICK

HERMAN MELVILLE

A Penguin Life

A LIPPER / VIKING BOOK

VIKING
Published by the Penguin Group
Penguin Putnam Inc., 375 Hudson Street,
New York, New York 10014, U.S.A.
Penguin Books Ltd, 27 Wrights Lane, London W8 5TZ, England
Penguin Books Australia Ltd, Ringwood, Victoria, Australia
Penguin Books Canada Ltd, 10 Alcorn Avenue,
Toronto, Ontario, Canada M4V 3B2
Penguin Books (N.Z.) Ltd, 182–190 Wairau Road,
Auckland 10, New Zealand

Penguin Books Ltd, Registered Offices:
Harmondsworth, Middlesex, England

First published in 2000 by Viking Penguin,
a member of Penguin Putnam Inc.

1   3   5   7   9   10   8   6   4   2

LIBRARY OF CONGRESS CATALOGING IN PUBLICATION DATA
Hardwick, Elizabeth
Herman Melville / Elizabeth Hardwick.
p. cm.–(Penguin lives series)
"A Lipper/Viking book."
ISBN 0-670-89158-4
1. Melville, Herman, 1819–1891.   2. Novelists, American–
19th century–Biography.
I. Title.   II. Series
PS2386.H34 2000
813'.3–dc21   00–036510

This book is printed on acid-free paper
∞

Printed in the United States of America
Set in Baskerville Book
Designed by Francesca Belanger

To H.L. and to the memory of R.T.S.L.

CONTENTS

HERMAN MELVILLE

Whaling

HERMAN MELVILLE: sound the name and it's to be the romance of the sea, the vast, mysterious waters for which a thousand adjectives cannot suffice. Its mystical vibrations, the great oceans "holy" for the Persians, a deity for the Greeks; forbidden seas, passage to barbarous coasts—a scattering of Melville's words for the urge to know the sparkling waters and their roll-on beauty and, when angry, their powerful, treacherous indifference to the floundering boat and the hapless mariners.

The sea and the Whale, the Leviathan, monarch of the deep, preternatural immensity, exorbitant appetite, "a barrel of herrings in his belly"; hairless blubber, horizontal tail—the lure of the whale himself, his island bulk, "one grand hooded phantom, like a snow hill in the air." We take Melville at his word, for he is the historian, the biographer of the whale; the Sperm Whale with its precious oils and bones, the shy Fin Back, the Hyena Whale, the Right Whale, the Killer Whale. Cetology—a challenge to the mind and soul; the whale a fish for Melville, not a mammal, however warm-blooded the great one may be.

To go from contemplation of the *Whale* to *Whaling* is a brute descension should youthful wanderlust see the world by this dark contract, by signing on. It's a floating abattoir, an abysmal duty to sight one or a group coming up for air, to man the boats hanging on the ship's side and in the boiling splash of the water with appalling human effort match the whale's torrential struggle with the flying spears. Caught, lashed to the boat's side, gallons and gallons of blood and the sharks competing. There it is, the huge, dying cargo, then dead, ready for "cutting in." The thick blubber to be stripped off, not in sections but as a blanket. "Now as the blubber envelopes the whale precisely as an orange is sometimes stripped by spiralizing it . . . for a moment or two the prodigious blood-dripping mass sways to and fro as if let down from the sky."

Captured, hacked off, the huge, neckless head of the whale, its decapitation in a whaler looked on as a precious crown, if you like, for its spermaceti, tons of oil, and soothing ambergris; oil boiled to make candles, give light in the darkness; and somewhere in the slaughter, bones for Ahab's leg, for corsets, scrimshaw trinkets; many domestic refinements and scents there in the blood and guts. The texture of the slabs is not quite felicitous for food, Melville tells us, although it was eaten by the early hunters, by the Eskimo, and by the second mate, Stubbs, on the *Pequod,* who attacks in a comical chapter several huge whale steaks with a personal relishing.

The whaler, the exploitation of the dead beast, is not a youthful, romantic adventure of bracing experience. So many of one's companions have come sulking away, address unknown, from howling creditors, accusing wives, alert policemen, beggary on shore. Except for a few of a sensibility refined like Melville's own, it is day and night, months, years with the thoroughly ruined, the outcasts, the drunken and diseased, and here and there a welcome ordinary sailor of harmless eccentricity and vagrant skills.

In Melville's novels before *Moby-Dick,* to sign on for work on shipboard is soon to plot an escape no matter what the risk. The whale itself, the idea of it, does not reach its apotheosis until the imaginary voyage on the *Pequod,* where, of necessity, for the art of the book, the terms of the whaling life will offer a sort of advancement, an upgrading. From a chapter in *Moby-Dick* with the title "The Advocate":

> Doubtless one leading reason why the world declines honoring us whalemen, is this: they think that, at best, our vocation amounts to a butchering sort of business; and that when actively engaged therein, we are surrounded by all manner of defilements. Butchers we are, that is true. But butchers also, and butchers of the bloodiest badge have been all Martial Commanders whom the world invariably delights to honor . . . what disordered slippery decks of a whale-ship are comparable to the unspeakable carrion of those battle-fields from which so many soldiers return to drink in all ladies' plaudits?

Then he goes on to list the advantages to mankind brought by the whaling industry: "the tapers, lamps, and candles that burn round the globe, burn, as before so many shrines, to our glory!" And the whaleship as an instrument of exploration: "For many years past the whale-ship has been the pioneer in ferreting out the remotest and least-known parts of the earth. She has explored seas and archipelagoes which had no chart, where no Cook or Vancouver had ever sailed." And in what we can read as a facetious "Postscript"—his title—he asserts the advantage of the pomade, the hair oil, on the head of the king at his coronation, "even as a head of salad. . . . Certainly it cannot be olive oil, nor macassar oil, nor castor oil, nor bear's oil, nor train oil, nor cod-liver oil. What then can it possibly be, but sperm oil in its unmanufactored, unpolluted state, the sweetest of all oils?"

This is the mood of *Moby-Dick* and the whaler *Pequod,* a death ship but not a vessel of mundane commercial ferocity. The aim is, under Captain Ahab, only incidentally, if that, bound to fill vats with oil and return to Nantucket with household and family income. It's a voyage of arcane personal vindication, the death of the White Whale in payment or vengeance for the leg he has taken from Ahab. A magical plot of great strangeness and something of the grandeur of historic kings in battle. From the *Pequod,* Melville does not propose an escape to islands as in his other sea novels. It is to be an intense plot and a history of the whale and whaling, given in encyclopedic detail and written with a wild, inexhaustible language coming in a rush like waves, thereby honoring the deadly enterprise.

"If at my death, my executors, or more properly my creditors, find any precious MSS. in my desk, then there I prospectively ascribe all the honor and glory to whaling; for a whale-ship was my Yale College and my Harvard." Not quite, indeed not at all, far from it. Melville is the most bookish of writers, a tireless midnight student. He has read and uses everything: Shakespeare, the Bible, Sir Thomas Browne, the epic *Lusiads* by the Portuguese poet Camoëns, national history, marine history, natural history, zoology.

The chapter "Cetology" is divided into a sort of mock academic shape; the Folio Whale, the Octavo Whale, the Duodecimo Whale. This expansiveness of information is necessary for a public that knows little of the whale and whaling and has its source in the same instructive purpose as Zola on coal mining in *Germinal*.

But Melville's method of information is an extravagant, poetic language, an exalted factuality:

> The Fin-Back is not gregarious. He seems a whale-hater, as some men are man-haters. Very shy; always going solitary . . . this leviathan seems the banished and unconquerable Cain of his race, bearing for his mark that style upon his back.

In the commentaries about Melville there is considerable sentiment about sailing and the oceans and Melville himself as a sea-struck vagabond, a land-bred youth with a lust for wanderings. Although he didn't know it at the time, the sea was to give him his art, his occupation, but the actual romance of landscape, the sun on the waves, the stars at night, are nearly always mixed with the brutality of life on board. And the art that saved him, the discovery of his genius, was a sort of Grub Street, a book a year, sometimes two. And not altogether different from

Elizabeth Hardwick

Macaulay's description of "the writing game" at the time of Doctor Johnson:

> Even an author whose works were established, and whose works were popular, such as author Thomson, whose *Seasons* was in every library, such an author as Fielding, whose *Pasquin* had had a greater run than any drama since *The Beggar's Opera,* was sometimes glad to obtain by pawning his best coat, the means of dining on tripe at a cookshop underground, where he could wipe his hands, after a greasy meal, on the back of a Newfoundland dog.

And Melville himself, although slaving away in a respectable house in Manhattan and in the luxuriant meadows of a pleasant town in western Massachusetts, might, in his obscure and never quite assimilated nature, have preferred life in the underground cookshop with the Newfoundland dog.

New York

THE POET OF THE SEA, the youthful observer of ships and enchanted islands; there's that and Ishmael washed up in the savage's coffin, a lone survivor. And down the years, more than a century later, so much of the writer had lain submerged that *poor* Melville seems to come to mind when we think of this profligate benefactor of our literature.

There is a forlorn accent shadowing the great energy of his thought and imagination. There is a rueful dignity in his life and personal manner, and sometimes a startling abandonment of propriety on the pages. He was not a gifted angel winging up from the streets, the slums of the great metropolis Manhattan. Instead, he was as well-born as any American of his time. And yet funds were scarce and scanty throughout his youth and not always forthcoming for one who published ten works of fiction in eleven years before giving up to spend nineteen years as a customs inspector down on the Battery, before dying at the age of seventy-two.

There have been poorer writers who died younger than Melville; indeed, *poor* Melville is a sigh not only for the bill collector at the door and the neglect of his work but also for the sense we have of a haunted and haunting man. Who was he? Godless or God-seeking? Mystic or realist? Natural husband and father or one swimming in oceanic homoerotic yearnings? Disappointed, restless, or near to madness? The gorgeous phantasmagoria, *Moby-Dick:* Who can finally know the whole of Melville's intention in the creation of the wild gladiators, Captain Ahab and the White Whale?

He is elusive, the facts of his life only a frame, as perhaps they are for the honored, much-studied dead, as well as for the obscure. This often unhappy man knew many happy days; or was it that this more or less settled gentleman had periods of desolation? All is true, if you like. There was a fireside and a dinner table, the admirable Elizabeth Shaw Melville as a wife, two sons and two daughters.

We think back on neglected artists and esteem the reclamation, the fresh discovery that comes to some in the shape of books, interpretations, exegeses of an almost violent exuberance, a search of crevice and cranny. There will be analysis that returns to the womb of the mother or to the longing for the love of the lost father. Secrets of the tomb may lie in verbal ambiguities, calling for a dictionary excavation of root and interesting doubleness. Melville was unearthed in the 1920s, the whole skeleton, as it were, put under the floodlights, a penetrating radar giving the bones a voluptuous rebirth. This anthropological honor by so many gifted readers at last placed Melville in the high regard earned by his early creative energy and by the fantastic explosion of genius in *Moby-Dick.*

Herman Melville

He is a New Yorker, born in 1819, like another New Yorker, Walt Whitman; and dying together, or nearly— Melville, 1891, and Whitman, 1892. They did not meet on the Manhattan waterfront in a bardic salute or some other recognition; however, Whitman wrote favorable reviews of *Typee* and *Omoo* in the *Brooklyn Eagle*. Birth on Pearl Street, down near the Battery on the Hudson River, with the big ships coming in and going out, is a romantic beginning for Melville's challenging career. The landscape of his art is to be the open sea surging around the prison that is a lone boat under sail, with its sundry human cargo, its presumptuous mission to capture and strip the largest animal in nature. It is a youthful escape to a cannibal island, a slave-ship mutiny, a derangement at sea with catastrophic finalities. On land, a Gothic New York family, a picaresque masquerade, a loner in a Wall Street office.

Every day for twenty years, 1846–1866, it was his aim and duty to make a living for himself and his family. The gods were with him at the beginning, but they lost interest after a time, as the capricious spirits will. He was published and sold less and less as the years went on; he was known as a man of letters but not much read. Resignation? Writing poems at night, yes, but during those nights his state was often such that his wife thought him deranged and considered a separation. His son, Malcolm, his firstborn, put a pistol to his head. The son was eighteen years old and had incurred the displeasure of his father by the typical defaults of young men; drinking, staying out late. Stanwix, the second son, died of tuberculosis out in California at the age of thirty-five. And there is the author of *Moby-Dick,* at the age of forty-seven, looking out on the Hudson not as a dreaming youth but as a clerk for hire in the waterfront shed, weighing goods for tax.

W. H. Auden's poem on Melville:

> But it was the gale had blown him
> Past the Cape Horn of sensible success
> Which cries: "This rock is Eden. Shipwreck here."

Hart Crane: "At Melville's Tomb." (The actual tomb is an unremarkable one in a cemetery in the Bronx.)

> Compass, quadrant and sextant contrive
> No farther tides . . . High in the azure steeps
> Monody shall not wake the mariner.
> This fabulous shadow only the sea keeps.

Melville's family: In the way distinction was measured at the time, he was as well connected as any of the New Englanders of the "flowering" period. The Melvilles were a good Boston family, and his mother was Maria Gansevoort, solid Dutch patroons of Albany. Despite that, the family history is of a somewhat unbalancing kind, especially on the Melville side. Things should have gone better with them, and they give the feeling of a defeated nation or, more exactly, of certain European families with a fading title, handicapped by the sweep of history or by maladaptation. Thomas Melville, grandfather, married Pricilla Scollay, and no doubt her name decorates Boston's

Scollay Square, as does the name Gansevoort serve the downtown Manhattan street where Herman worked. He once, with a certain wryness, asked a passerby where the name came from. He was told it must have been some family that once bought property around there.

The Melvilles were a Boston merchant family who could claim the sort of heraldic honor that to this day, two centuries later, keeps the prideful busy with the genealogists; that is, service in the American Revolution. Major Thomas Melville was down at Boston Harbor in 1773 and with other young men boarded the ships of the East India Company and dumped their cargo of tea into the water. A handful of tea leaves, or what were thought to be, passed down to the heirs. This ancestor, grandfather, was a graduate of Princeton, fought at Bunker Hill, and was appointed naval officer of the port of Boston. Removed by a change of political administrations, he seemed content to spend his later years in the Boston Custom House.

(The Custom House, a fateful ring in American literature. Hawthorne, in his three years' service at the establishment in Salem, could paint some amusing portraits of the old fellows dozing through the day. But it was a scene of blinding tedium: "In view of my previous weariness of office, and vague thoughts of resignation, my fortune somewhat resembled that of a person who should entertain an idea of committing suicide, and, altogether beyond his hopes, meet with the good hap to be murdered.")

Old Major Melville, without artistic ambitions, seemed to take his Custom House with good humor as a sort of government pension. He was a "figure" about Boston, a war hero of the Revolution, volunteer firefighter, eccentrically dressed in a three-cornered hat and knee breeches. Daniel Webster delivered his funeral oration. Like other families, proud of early residence in the United States, they nevertheless had to come from somewhere. The Melvilles of America arrived from Scotland and along the way back claimed descent from the Scotch nobility, the family of the earl of Melvill and Leven, a connection much valued and often pronounced by Allan Melville, Herman's father.

Melville's mother was Maria Gansevoort of Albany, from prominent Dutch early settlers. Her father, Colonel Peter Gansevoort, was also a hero in the Revolution, fighting at Fort Stanwix against the Indian and Tory troops. This was a contest cruel and yet colorful in the historical record. Joseph Brant, a Mohawk chieftain who had converted to Christianity, in a reversal returned to lead his tribe in conjunction with the British against the Americans. The Indians stormed a fortress but were driven back to another position, where they massacred whites. Colonel Gansevoort, in retaliation, set fire to native villages, destroyed their crops, and held Fort Stanwix. Naming their son after the battle indicates that Herman Melville and his wife honored the position of the family in history, even if the slaughter on both sides makes Fort Stanwix a dubious honor.

The Gansevoorts fared better than the Melvilles, who seemed to have a genetic disposition to bankruptcy. After the Revolution, the Gansevoorts prospered, received land grants in upstate New York, near Lake George, and married into the Hudson Valley aristocracy. Allan Melville, the father of Herman Melville: As a young man he had planned a venture into real-estate investment with Peter Gansevoort of Albany and Lemuel Shaw, a Boston friend. The business arrangement, sadly foretelling of Allan's financial biography, did not come about, but he married Peter's sister, Maria Gansevoort. Lemuel Shaw, later chief justice of the Massachusetts Supreme Court, became engaged to Nancy Melville, Allan Melville's sister, who died before the marriage, and later his daughter, Elizabeth, was to be the wife of Herman Melville. The fraternal relationship was a felicitous one even though the Melvilles were to become a drain on the bank accounts of the Gansevoorts and Shaws. In a remarkably generous and forgiving spirit, Judge Shaw was the bountiful presence, a friendly deity, in Herman's life. Over and over, again and again, it is to be "on a loan from Judge Shaw" and "paid for by Judge Shaw."

Herman's father, Allan Melville, one of eleven children, appears to have been a dashing, good-natured, sophisticated young man, altogether promising. He had been a good student in the West Boston School and went off to Paris under the wing of his older brother, Thomas, learned French well, and set himself up in Albany and Boston in a dry-goods importing business. He moved from Boston to New York in the belief that it would be more profitable for the fashionable goods he wished to offer. The family settled on Pearl Street, where Herman was born. Soon after, they moved to a "better address" on Courtland Street and then on to 33 Bleecker Street. More children, more deals, each turn begun in hope on borrowed capital. Hard times brought a shrinkage in the demand for laces and velvets and European decorative wares, with the result that Allan Melville could not pay the creditors, who were distressingly rude about it.

Mark Twain on the entrepreneurial mind: Yesterday I didn't have a nickel and today I owe a million dollars. The Melville family embarked on trade dreams that perhaps were modest enough in the America of the 1820s, when one encounters the wildly expansive imagination of Mrs. Trollope in the construction of her Bazaar in the city of Cincinnati. An unaccountable bit of grandiosity the building was: "taken in part from the Mosque of St. Athanese in Egypt," with elaborate colonnades and a ballroom in "the style of the Alhambra, the celebrated palace of the Moorish kings in Granada." Mrs. Trollope, destitute, fled the country, returned to England to make her fortune writing *Domestic Manners of the Americans*. A revenge, perhaps, at least against the idea that everything in the United States turned to gold.

Meanwhile, Allan Melville's older brother, Thomas, who had brought him to Paris and to acquaintance with the French language and with certain interesting Continental figures of the time, was suddenly cast down from his attractive and promising life by the family's inclination to fall into dramatic insolvency. Thomas had succeeded in the Paris banking world and married the adopted niece of Madame Récamier's husband. He was forced to return to Massachusetts with his French wife and six children, the youngest of whom, along with the mother, died in Pittsfield, where Thomas took over the farm bought by the elder Melville. Pittsfield was the pleasure of Herman Melville's youth, and later, with, as ever, a loan from Judge Shaw, he bought a house in the neighborhood and lived there for thirteen years before returning to New York. *Moby-Dick* was written in Pittsfield, in the house he named Arrowhead.

Thomas, Herman Melville's uncle, married a widow, and together they had eight children, which meant thirteen in all to be taken care of by the farm. Thomas appeared to have been an industrious gentleman farmer, managing the fields in a creditable manner. However, bank loans and mortgage payments accumulated, and the crops, in their eternal unreliability, frequently failed to do so. Frantic calls for new loans to cover payments on old loans. The old Melville and Judge Shaw, who had signed previous notes, failed to respond to yet another financial rescue, and as a consequence they were later sued by the bank, and the friendly orator Daniel Webster argued for the defense. Thomas went to jail for four months, until his father relented and bailed him out. Allan Melville was somewhat pompous about his brother's delinquencies, perhaps because they interfered for a time with his own solution to financial distress.

Allan and his wife, Maria, settled in Manhattan as they were, had to consider the city's way of defining one by an address, and thus they kept on the move, geographically and socially. So it was to be a large house on Broadway. Maria was not a Gansevoort for nothing and was serious in the matter of her social rights or preferences. Herman Melville's youth was spent going from a nice house to a nicer house and then quite soon moving down once more. More children were born, and an unsteady propriety was somehow assumed, with Gansevoort and Herman enrolled in the Columbia Grammar School, the best in the city. Still, dollars and cents, with their arrogant reality, prevailed, and the family was forced to flee New York in financial disgrace. Flee for Albany, the Gansevoort principality. There the father tried to set up a fur-and-cap shop, but he was as always underfunded. That too collapsed.

Allan Melville met his death at age fifty in a miserably unfortunate manner, the last days adding a blight to the sadness of death itself. He came down with severe fevers, a violent pneumonia with its accompanying sweats and deliriums. In about three weeks he was dead. The restless, unabating deliriums caused those attending and visiting to believe that he had gone mad, that he died as a *maniac*. Pneumonia before the discovery of penicillin was a devastating disease, and whether the ravings, the deliriums, could be considered a *clinical* madness rather than the lingering disorientation of the illness we might doubt today.

Herman Melville was thirteen years old at the time of his father's death. His early life had the vivacity and vitality of his brothers and sisters, cousins, journeys with his father, and visits to the farm in Pittsfield. Just how the financial distresses played out at the fireside in the relations between husband and wife naturally cannot be known. But it seems to have been a mutual struggle to keep afloat in the world, and perhaps the parents were allies. Maria Gansevoort Melville was not a thrifty housewife but a name-proud spender, and that would give her a certain collusion in the dizzy swings of fate. They shared the anxiety and, always, the hopes for rescue. She had the tradesmen at the door, the school bills, the rent due, all turning up with an ordained regularity. Money frenzy for breakfast along with pride and hope.

At the father's death, the problems of the grieving family became more and more crushing. Gone was the emotional energy of the father, the buying and selling warfare, the waiting for him to come home of an evening with the news, even the liveliness of the efforts to fight off defeat. Allan Melville was lovable, engaging, and forever promising or he could not have secured so much ill-advised credit.

Genteel poverty, an ambiguous condition, each contradiction feeding upon the other. The atmosphere of gentility arises in village life from the remembrance of things past created by birth, prosperity, an honorable reputation, even charm. Good manners, certain fine pieces of furniture or silver, still remaining. And above all, a feeling of entitlement, a treacherous companion that encourages debt. It is all expectation and dreaming. Ordinary townsfolk, working, drawing pay, slowly adding a wing to the house, dressing the children better; a sort of organic progress, if such should be available. For the Melville mother and father the inclination seemed to have been, when things looked promising, to rush into the buying of emblematic signatures they had known in the past—a better house, servants, good social placement for the children. So it ever went; a reluctance to practice economy and foresight. On the other hand, thrift is as unpleasant as poverty. Nothing to offer in daily life except reality.

In Albany, Maria's family radiance did not suffice with past and present creditors threatening. Gansevoort Melville, four years older than Herman, was set up with loans in his father's fur business, and for a time he had a striking success and became a man about town. But with a lurid repetitiveness, the business went into receivership, and Gansevoort was sent to New York to live with a friend and to study law. Even in the time of a family death, the intransigent load of litigation did not subside. The elder grandfather Melville lived a year longer than his son Allan; however, when the father's will was probated, it was learned that Allan's debts had been deducted from the father's estate. The creditors sued, as they will.

In Albany: unremitting black weather for the Melville household. The widow and her children were forced to sell much of their furniture and other effects and to escape in ignominy to a cheaper town, Lansingburgh, nearby. Herman for a period taught school, took an engineering degree at Lansingburgh Academy, failed to get a position, wrote some youthful sketches which were published in the local paper—and then, perhaps, we can say his true life began. However, the life he left behind, the losses, the grief, the instability, the helpless love of a helpless young man in a damaged family, marked his sensibility quite as much as the wanderlust, the strong grip of the sea, so often claimed as the defining aspect of his nature. In 1839 he signed on as a lowly cabin boy on the *St. Lawrence,* a merchant ship bound for a four-month trip to Liverpool. He was twenty years old.

Redburn

MELVILLE'S STATE OF MIND is revealed some years later with a purity of expressiveness in the novel *Redburn,* one of the most appealing and certainly the most personal of his works. He is said to have more or less disowned the book, more rather than less, since he claimed it was only "written for tobacco." Whether this is a serious misjudgment of his own work or a withdrawal, after the fact, from having shown his early experience of life without his notable reserve and distance is, of course, not clear. For a contemporary reader, Redburn, the grief-stricken youth, cast among the vicious, ruined men on the ship, walking the streets of Liverpool in the 1830s, even the meeting with the homosexual hustler Harry Bolton might have more interest than *Typee*'s breadfruit and coconut island and the nymph Fayaway. But it is only pertinent to think of *Redburn* on its own: a novel written after *Typee, Omoo,* and *Mardi* in the year 1849, ten years after he left Lansingburgh to go on his first voyage.

"Cold, bitter cold as December, and bleak as its blasts, seemed the world then to me; there is no misanthrope like a boy disappointed; and such was I, with the warm soul of me flogged out by adversity." Melville was not a boy when he joined the *St. Lawrence,* but the remembrance of his father and the last years seem in detail to represent his actual thoughts at the time. Despair, rooted in experience, in love of family and a young son's defenseless anxiety amid the tides of misfortune, leave their mark on his character and on his view of life. The opening pages are a profoundly moving poem to his dead father, to the memory of evenings in New York, talk around the fireside of the cities and sights of Europe, the treasures Allan brought home from Paris. There was a large bookcase filled with books, many in French, paintings and prints, furniture, pictures from natural history, including a whale "big as a ship, struck full of harpoons, and three boats sailing after it as fast as they could fly."

The sea, the traveler's passionate curiosity and longing: "Foreign associations bred in me a vague prophetic thought that I was fated, one day or another, to be a great voyager; and that just as my father used to entertain strange gentlemen over their wine after dinner, I would hereafter be telling my own adventures to an eager auditory." Most vivid in his memory was an intricately made glass ship brought home from Hamburg. The magical ship "fell from its perch the very day I left home to go to sea on this my first voyage." Things are fragile and subject to spots and stains, the rude damages of family life, but the utter shattering of the familiar glass beauty, named *La Reine,* adds another mournful accent, symbolic if you like, to the breakage in Melville's early life, if we consider these pages to be a recapitulation of the past feeling, as they appear to be.

Nothing in Melville is more beautifully expressed than the mood of early sorrow in the forlorn passage at the opening of *Redburn*. It brings to mind the extraordinarily affecting last word in *Moby-Dick:* The word is *orphan.*

> I had learned to think much and bitterly before my time . . . talk not of the bitterness of middle-age and after life; a boy can feel all that and much more, when upon his young soul the mildew has fallen; and the fruit, which with others is only blasted after ripeness, with him is nipped in the first blossom and bud. And never again can such blights be made good; they strike too deep, and leave such a scar that the air of Paradise might not erase it.

"Such blights that can never be made good," the chastening of experience, the deathbed struggle of his father, his mother an improvident widow, his own straggling lack of a future occupation; all of these burdens formed Melville's early sense of the ambiguity, the chaos of life, quite as much as the Dutch Reform Calvinism of his mother, and underlined his surpassing sympathy for the pagan, the ignorant, even the evil. The black-comedy subtitle of *Redburn* is *Son-of-a-Gentleman, in the Merchant Service.* A friend, seeing off the young recruit, tells the captain to take good care of him, since his uncle is a senator and the boy's father had crossed the ocean many times on important business. On shore the captain appeared to take this information in an agreeable manner, but once at sea he violently spurns the boy's misbegotten idea of paying a friendly visit to his cabin. In the midst of young Redburn's good manners and proper upbringing, his being the son of a Melville and a Gansevoort is a grotesque irrelevance; the truth of his life as others see it is his abject pennilessness, his humbling, ragged clothes. He will be homesick, and yet the anonymity, the nakedness of background, are not unwelcome. The ocean is an escape and not a practical decision, not a job from which a young man could send money home to honor a struggling family. It is common in Melville's seagoing stories to find that once back in port, the crew will be robbed of its miserable wages by the inspired accounting chicanery of the captain and the owners. Melville's first voyage did nothing to deflect the furtive position of his family when the importunate grocer, landlord, or dressmaker knocked on the door.

In *Redburn,* on board the *Highlander,* as the fictional ship is named, there is a man named Jackson, one of the most loathsome portraits in Melville's fiction. About him, a descriptive vocabulary of depravity is summoned with a special intensity. Yellow as a gamboge, bald except for hair behind his ears that looked like a worn-out shoe brush, nose broken down the middle, a squinting eye, the foul lees and dregs of a man. Jackson is wasting away from his "infamous vices," venereal disease, and yet he is, or was, the best seaman on board, a bully feared by all the men, this "wolf or starved tiger," with his "deep, subtle, infernal looking eye." He had been at sea since the age of eight and

"had passed through every kind of dissipation and abandonment in the worst parts of the world." He told "with
relish" of having crewed on a slave ship where the slaves
were "stowed like logs and the suffocated were unmana-
cled thrown overboard."

Jackson's end comes on the return voyage when the
ship is off Cape Cod. He orders, "Haul out to windward!"
and with a torrent of blood gushing from his lungs, falls
into the sea. Melville has imagined this ruined man with a
visual and moral brilliance, shown his repellent body with
an awful precision, and yet consider his concluding feelings about the miserable Jackson:

> He was a Cain afloat, branded on his yellow brow with
> some inscrutable curse and going about corrupting and
> searing every heart that beat near him. But there was
> more woe than wickedness about the man; his wicked-
> ness seemed to spring from his woe; and for all his
> hideousness, there was that in his eye at times that was
> ineffably pitiable and touching; and though there were
> moments when I almost hated this Jackson, yet I have
> pitied no man as I pitied him.

Jackson's woe, Ahab's "close-coiled woe," and Melville's woe in his youth. *Redburn* was written ten years after the first journey, after the publication of the three
previous books. It is a return to his voyage on the *St.
Lawrence,* but he has made Redburn a boy, a lad, a shabby
waif, even though when he himself set sail he was twenty

years old and there is no reason to believe he came on in tatters like the men prowling the waterfront: homeless, illiterate, and wasted. Still, when Melville looked back, he did so as a writer and magically created Redburn for the purposes of a kind of fiction and for his memories of Liverpool, his first foreign city. The personal accent of the opening pages of grief and forlornness are so striking that they may be read as a memory of the thirteen-year-old Melville at the time of his father's death. Redburn carries his father's out-of-date guide to Liverpool and walks the streets in a mood of filial homage. "How differently my father must have appeared; perhaps in a blue coat, buff vest, and Hessian boots; and little did he think, that a son of his would ever visit Liverpool as a poor friendless sailor-boy." What Melville's eye perceives and how his intelligence judges it were quite apart from the conventional sight-seeing of the charming dandy, his father. Instead, on a Liverpool street called Launcelott's-Hey, among the dreary, dingy warehouses, Redburn hears a feeble wail that leads to a searing dirge.

In a cellar beneath the old warehouse, he saw a figure who "had been a woman." On her livid breast there were two shrunken things "like children." They had crawled into the space to die. The sailor inquires about the terrible sight, questions ragged, desperate old women in the alleys. The old, beggarly people, destitute themselves, are contemptuous of the ghastly family group who have had nothing to eat for three days. A policeman shrugs; the lady at Redburn's rooming house refuses help; the cook, when asked for food, "broke out in a storm of swearing." Redburn snatches some bread and cheese and drops it down the vault. Frail hands grasped at the food but were too weak to catch hold. There is a murmuring sound asking for "something faintly like water," and Redburn runs to a tavern for a pitcher but is refused unless he pays for it; he cannot. In his tarpaulin hat he draws water from Boodle Hydrants and returns to the vault.

> The two girls drank out of the hat together; looking up at me with an unalterable, idiotic expression, that almost made me faint. The woman spoke not a word and did not stir. . . . I tried to lift the woman's head; but feeble as she was, she seemed bent upon holding it down. Observing her arms still clasped upon her bosom, and that something seemed hidden among the rags there, a thought crossed my mind, which impelled me forcibly to withdraw her hands for a moment; then I caught a glimpse of a meager little babe, the lower part of its body thrust into an old bonnet. Its face was dazzlingly white, but the closed eyes looked like balls of indigo. It must have been dead for some hours. . . . when I went to dinner I hurried into Launcelott's-Hey, where I found that the vault was empty. In place of the women and children, a heap of quick-lime was glistening.

The scene of tragic extremity is composed with a rhetorical brilliance: the dying children with "eyes and lips, and ears *like any queen*"; with hearts which, "though they did not bound with blood, yet beat with a dull, dead ache that was their life"; and the dramatic insertion of pushing the mother's arm aside to reveal yet another being, a dead baby; and the return the next day to find the hole filled with *glistening* quicklime. Here we have the last rites, a gravestone offered for a street burial, a requiem for a hole in Launcelott's-Hey—the majestic reverence of Herman Melville.

Redburn visits the noted sights of Liverpool, hears the Chartist soapbox orators, street singers, men selling verses on current murders and other happenings; pawnshops, the impoverished dredging of the river for bits of rope, the rush of life that brings to mind Dickens and also Mayhew's study of the obscure populace in *London Labour and the London Poor*. Throughout Melville's writing's there is a liberality of mind, a freedom from vulgar superstition, occasions again and again for an oratorical insertion of enlightened opinion. Note a side glance in Liverpool, written in the year 1849:

> Three or four times, I encountered our black steward, dressed very handsomely, and walking arm in arm with a good-looking English woman. In New York, such a couple would have been mobbed in three minutes; and the steward would have been lucky to have escaped with whole limbs. Owing to the friendly reception extended to them, and the unwonted immunities they enjoy in Liverpool, the black cooks and stewards on American ships are very much attached to the place and like to make voyages to it. . . . at first I was surprised that a

colored man should be treated as he is in this town; but a little reflection showed that, after all, it was but recognizing his claims to humanity and normal equality; so that, in some things we Americans leave to other countries the carrying out of the principle that stands at the head of our Declaration of Independence.

Sentiment and agitation for the emancipation of the slaves was common enough in the Northeast at the time, but Melville's "reflection" was a stretch of opinion to include the right of a black man and a white woman to mingle as they wished socially and, he seems to be saying, sexually. When the Civil War arrived, Melville followed it with some distress of spirit about the slaughter. Around the conflict he wrote, in *Battle Pieces and Aspects of the War,* the finest of his poems.

On the docks Redburn observes the immigrants crowding onto the ships to make their way to America.* Again Melville speaks:

There was hardly anything I witnessed in the docks that interested me more than the German emigrants who come on board the large New York ships several days

*Philip Rahv in a collection of essays, *Discovery of Europe,* reprints passages from *Redburn* and comments about the description of the German emigrants. "An extraordinarily moving celebration of the hopes lodged in the New World and one of the noblest pleas in our literature for the extinction of national hatreds and racial prejudice."

before their sailing, to make everything comfortable ere starting. . . . And among these sober Germans, my country counts the most orderly and valuable of her foreign population. . . . There is something in the contemplation of the mode in which America has been settled that, in a noble breast, should forever extinguish prejudices or national dislikes. . . . You cannot spill a drop of American blood without spilling the blood of the whole world. . . . Our blood is as the flood of the Amazon, made up of a thousand currents all pouring into one. We are not a nation, so much as a world; . . . we are without father or mother.

The last pages of *Redburn* introduce the ineffable Harry Bolton, a young Englishman met on the Liverpool docks. Bolton is perfectly formed, "with curling hair and silken muscles . . . his complexion was a mantling brunette, feminine as a girl's; his feet were small; his hands were white; and his eyes were large, black and womanly; and, poetry aside, his voice was as the sound of a harp." A warm friendship develops, and in the fiction Redburn and Bolton go off to London together, although there is no evidence that such a trip was made at the time. In London there is a remarkable visit to a male brothel—a strange, fastidiously observed, rococo urban landscape unlike any other dramatic intrusion in Melville's writings or in American literature at the time.

Some commentators speculate that Melville's dislike of *Redburn* was owing to his subsequent realization that he had exposed his own homoerotic longings. Whatever his unconscious or privately acknowledged feeling may have been, Melville was innocent of the instinct for self-protection on the page. The readers of his own time, the publishers and booksellers, do not seem to have paused before the enthusiastic and relishing adjectives surrounding male beauty. Hershel Parker's monumental biography has unearthed the reviews of *Redburn* and quotes a mention of the extraordinarily noticeable pages about Harry Bolton. "A dash of romance thrown in amongst the clutter of familiar and homely incidents" is the quotation; impossible to parse except as an instance of the relaxed language and hasty reading of reviewers for the press. The "gay" Melville took many decades to appear; and out of respect for the tides of the time it seems useful to gather the beautiful young men together in a later chapter for speculation.

The *St. Lawrence* made its way home to a berth on Wall Street, and Melville, in October 1839, after four months away, arrived back in Lansingburgh and was to find a dismal, mortifying situation. Creditors everywhere, Maria Melville insisting on yet another saving packet of money from her brothers, who were insisting they could not afford it. Herman was sent to Albany to make a degrading plea to Peter Gansevoort. In life it is common to find persons in truth *absolutely broke,* and yet there they are the next day buying the newspapers; and so it went with the Melvilles and their hanging on, bleeding. Herman got a position teaching school in the village of Greenbush, thirteen miles away, miles which, for economy, he had to cover on foot if he wished to go home. The school, as if in a maniacal laughter, ran out of money and could not pay the salaries, and that was the end of that.

Thomas Melville, the uncle of the Paris triumph and the Pittsfield disaster, was now living in Galena, Illinois. Here with a friend, Eli Fly, Melville went to more or less check things out in the West, that promising prairie, the wild, vast, beckoning frontier of the imagination as well as of the nation. The two friends traveled by boat on the Erie Canal, taking in Buffalo, Toledo, Detroit, and Chicago, all to enhance and perhaps to suggest the plot of *The Confidence-Man.* In *Moby-Dick,* Ishmael explains what canallers, the men managing the Erie boats, might be, revealing once more a genius for memory along with the excited eloquence about the American landscape.

> For in their interflowing aggregate, those grand fresh-water seas of ours—Erie, and Ontario, and Huron, and Superior, and Michigan,—possess an ocean-like expansiveness, with many of the ocean's noblest traits; with many of its rimmed varieties of races and of climes. . . . they have heard the fleet thunderings of naval victories; at intervals, they yield their beaches to the wild barbarians, whose red painted faces flash from out their peltry wigwams; for leagues and leagues are flanked by ancient and unentered forests, where the gaunt pines stand like serried lines of Kings in Gothic genealogies. . . . they mirror the paved capital of Buffalo and Cleveland, as well as Winnebago villages; they float alike the full-rigged merchant ship, the armed cruiser of the State, the steamer and the beach canoe. . . .

In Illinois, Melville would find his uncle Thomas, contrary to the wisdom of going West in search of fortune, living in a very reduced condition. Uncle Thomas, blighted, unlucky, felonious, impetuous loser, has the fate of a character in a novel rather than an actor in the biography of a novelist. Although Herman may not have been aware of it, his uncle, while clerking for a man named Hezekiah Gear, had been found taking money from the till. He was fired but not publicly exposed, and there he was taking odd jobs, blaming the national economy for his depressed plight, and moving into a precarious old age. The summer was not a loss for the travelers, but only a more careless mind than Melville's could have faced the decay of his uncle without personal and family grief.

A year and a half after returning from the voyage to Liverpool, after the trip to the Middle West, after looking for work in New York City, Melville signed on a whaling ship for what was to have been a four-year term. He might have entered the law as his older brother, Gansevoort, and his younger brother, Allan, would do. His intelligence and remarkable talent for self-education would have opened any door for him if he had wanted doors to open, as perhaps he did not. Going to sea was an acceptable decision in the America of the 1840s; it was a career open to talent and, more strikingly, open to lack of talent. In Melville's family, a number had followed that route, sometimes with unprofitable results. A Gansevoort cousin perished in a shipwreck; another was sent home with a venereal disease, only to return to service and to go down with the ship. Thomas Melville, the son of the out-of-pocket Uncle Tom, beat up a shipmate, was reprimanded, survived to get cholera and to go down with the ship.

These family men had sailed as officers, but Herman sailed as a common seaman. And indeed it is a stretch to imagine him as an officer taking on the assumptions and practice of authority over others; that "sultanism," as he called it, was abhorrent to him. Still, everyone knew that a whaling ship was the abyss of misery. His experience in *Redburn* had the advantage of being only four months and of landing in the city of Liverpool, but it was a gruesome extension of knowledge. A drunken sailor in delirium jumped overboard to the indifference of his mates; the *St. Lawrence* passed a wrecked ship with three men "who had lashed themselves to the taffrail for safety, but must have famished," passed without stopping; as Melville's own ship leaves port, a vile smell reveals that a dead man had been surreptitiously sneaked into one of the bunks. In any case, Melville decided to leave land, to escape. For what? Perhaps a nagging irresolution about his future, a melancholy assessment of the present, guilt for not being able to assist his mother, his sisters, his younger brother. And on the merchant ship he had come away with a memory of the pleasure in learning what it meant to work at sea.

Typee

ON JANUARY 3, 1841, Melville sailed from New Bedford as a common seaman on the maiden voyage of the whaler *Acushnet*. He was not quite twenty-two years old. Inevitably, the life on the whaler was marked by a capricious wretchedness, and he deserted after a year and a half. There was some sighting of whales, some capturing, but Melville does not seriously consider the matter. He passed the coasts of Brazil, Chile, Peru, and the Galápagos, and when they sailed into the bay of Nukuhieva in the Marguesas Islands, he "ran away," as he says. Thus we have *Typee*. The happy success of the book came not from the lure of the sea, not from the whales and whaling, but from the South Pacific tattooed bathing beauties, from a cannibal tribe as "host," from lazy, tropical amorousness, sleepy afternoons under the coconut tree.

Abandoning ship was a serious offense, and that sailors did so with a reckless defiance is a measure of the inhumanity aboard. The opening lines of *Typee:*

Six months at sea! Yes, reader, as I live, six months out of sight of land; cruising after the sperm whale beneath the scorching sun of the line, and tossed on the billows of the wide-rolling Pacific—the sky above, the sea around, and nothing else! Weeks and weeks ago our fresh provisions were all exhausted. There is not a sweet potato left; not a single yam.

The truants, if captured, could be put in irons; the site of the escape could be treacherous, even deadly; the harbor police unfriendly to the destitute, sea-worn human driftwood.

Melville is at some pains in *Typee* to justify the desertion, to give a legalistic grounding to his narrative. For his part, he had signed a contract binding him to serve for the period of the voyage. "But in all contracts, if one party fails to perform his share of the contract, is not the other virtually absolved from this liability?" His assertion is that the usage on board was tyrannical; the sick had been inhumanly neglected; the provisions had been doled out in scant allowance; and her cruises were unreasonably protracted. "The captain was the author of these abuses. . . ."

The command of the ship was under Captain Valentine Pease of Nantucket, and if it could be said that the ship was no more distressing and vicious than other whalers, it does not imply that the stupendous beauty of the Marguesas and the girls swimming like mythical mermaids alone prompted running away.

During the remainder of the *Acushnet*'s four-and-a-half-year maiden cruise, half of the crew would desert, one sailor would commit suicide, and two would die of venereal diseases. On the return voyage, her first and third mates jumped ship at Payta, Peru, leaving only eleven men on board when she arrived in port. In 1851, shortly after *Moby-Dick* was published, Melville learned that the *Acushnet* had run aground on St. Lawrence Island and broken up in heavy seas.*

Melville sailed on the *Acushnet* in January 1841 and did not return until October 3, 1844, a span of almost four years. These years form the landscape of his early books about the sea, along with *Redburn* from the earlier journey. As we read now, the years falsely take on the curious shape of a kind of writing assignment—this boat *Typee,* the next ship *Omoo,* and so on. They are written by a drifting first person narrator, an *I,* who will become Ishmael in *Moby-Dick,* as if at last to reveal how the *I* thought of himself. He thought of himself as an outcast, son of Abraham, but not in the royal line.

Melville is always a brilliant portraitist; here is the "squinting eye"; there a face like a "furnace of affliction"; in wild metaphors for the follies attendant upon position, the senior lieutenant on a U.S. Navy ship appears "like the father of a numerous family after getting up in his dressing gown and slippers, to quiet a daybreak tumult in his populous nursery." But he is not a painter of his own face in the mirror. The hell of the ship, the floggings, exhaustion, the depleted diet, the parsimony of sympathies, the igno-

---

*Robertson-Lorant, p. 106.

rance and obscenity: What marks did all of this leave on his deepest self?

He is a mystery, and perhaps, like Bartleby, the Scrivener, in a late story, "no materials exist for a full and satisfactory biography of this man." This port and that, the islands, the countries, "I had to travel to dispel all the sorceries gathered in my brain. On the sea which I loved, I saw the cross of consolation rise. I had been damned by the rainbow . . ." (Rimbaud). Rimbaud, deserting France for Africa, returned only to die; but we have Herman Melville, still a young man, back in upstate New York, going about in a suit and tie, sitting at his desk reviving his memories in a waterfall of words, images, metaphors, details of custom and tribe, heathen practices—a poetical anthropology.

He will need on the boats to find a companion. In *Typee,* a young sailor, Richard Tobias Greene, of Buffalo, New York, joins him in the daring escape. Ahead lies the beautiful Nukuheva with the seafowl, the man-of-war's hawk "with its blood-red bill and raven plumage," unexpected rocky cliffs "broken here and there in deep inlets" and "thickly wooded valleys," and many tales of cannibal tribes therein. To get out of sight of the *Acushnet* the two must climb steep cliffs, make their way through brambles and menacing thickets in a torrential downpour, suffer hunger and thirst, and all the while be ignorant about the habitants below. Cannibals or the more peaceable natives of Happar? The battle with the elements and the unfamiliar landscape is rendered with suspenseful mastery. At last they come down into the dreaded Typee valley, which, confounding rumor and false ethnography, is a surprisingly hospitable village.

More or less accurate happenings form a useful "plot." Melville has come down with fevers, weakness, and a painful infection of his leg that does not abate and makes him a sort of invalid—to be carried about and nursed as if in a primitive hospice. The aim of the two deserters had not been to hang out and do a bit of beachcombing. They want to board another ship, and Toby, as he is called in the book, does not linger, but with the guarded help of a duplicitous old white beachcomber, long on the island, makes his way to a boat anchored in the harbor. His intention is to return with medicine and help for Tommo, as Melville is named, to be carried off the island. The ship will not linger or return, and it was not known until *Typee* was published, by each whether the other had survived.

In the valley, Melville is alone of his kind, if one wants to put it so. He was not, as "a peep at Polynesian life" states, in residence for four months but for four weeks at the most and perhaps only three weeks. The excuse for this exaggeration is usually, by friendly commentators, thought to be due to a wish to give credence to his richly detailed documentation. In any case, there he was, crippled and weak and treated by the "savages" not only with elaborate courtesy but with an almost smothering attentiveness.

He is taken into an island family and especially watched over by the son, Kory-Kory, who, unlike the tall, handsome men visitors to the island had noted, is quite ugly to begin with and not improved by an atrocious choice of tattoos. His mother is the only person about who seems to do anything; she cooks, makes cloth, and dashes about looking for herbs. Except for Kory-Kory, the young men of the household are dissipated, good-for-nothing, "roystering blades of savages." The young ladies seem to swim and put flowers in their hair.

Kory-Kory is the custodian of Tommo's welfare, carrying him about on his back, feeding him, sleeping beside him. For reasons never quite clear, the islanders have a fierce determination to prevent Melville from leaving. The other native character to emerge in the narration is the beautiful, and only lightly tattooed, flower child Fayaway. She is devoted, "natural," filled with sympathetic tenderness for his leg pain and in "inexpressible sorrow" when at last he must leave. If Fayaway seems to us waiting for discovery in one of the sarong movies many, many years ahead, she might have appeared of more interest to the readers of the time. It's not clear that Melville intends to suggest a sexual relation with the island beauty; but later, after *Omoo,* after public resentment of his defamation of missionaries, after his attacks on the French role in Tahiti, a virulent assault on the author's morals, an assertion of profligacy with the innocent island girls, was mounted by Horace Greeley, the flamboyant newspaper editor and political journalist.

Fayaway, dropping her robe to display her beautiful body, is one thing, but the most curious scene in the book is an opaque passage with the description *"Kory-Kory strikes a light à la Typee."* A decayed stock of the hibiscus about "six feet in length and half as many inches in diameter" is rubbed together with a smaller stick to produce friction to make fire. However, the condition in which Kory-Kory finds himself during the operation suggests another type of friction.

> At first Kory-Kory goes to work quite leisurely, but gradually quickens his pace, and waxing warm in the employment, drives the stick furiously along the channel, plying his hands to and fro with amazing rapidity, the perspiration starting from every pore. As he approaches the climax of his effort, he pants and gasps for breath, and his eyes almost start from their sockets with the violence of his exertions. . . . This operation appeared to me to be the most laborious species of work performed in Typee. . . .

Part of the island is out of bounds, taboo, but as we go along toward the end of the book, it is clear that Melville, the ragtag observer, will be compelled to find the answer to charges of cannibalism. In a dramatic exposition it comes about, and, we assume, truthfully. Three packages covered in tappa, the native cloth, hanging from a pole excited his curiosity enough for him to force his way into the circle where the natives were examining them. The packages contained human heads: "Two of the three were heads of the islanders; but the third, to my horror, was that of a white man." A week or so later, the place is an uproar in a battle with the invading men of Happar, and the result is a great feast with the bodies of the slain enemy.

The time comes to manage an escape and to climb aboard another prettily named infernal whaler that will take him to *Omoo*. The ship is the *Lucy Ann* of Australia. It will be two years before Melville will be back home when the naval vessel, the *United States,* honored or trapped in *White-Jacket,* anchors in the Charlestown Navy Yard, outside Boston. His official release was several weeks later, but he did not immediately notify his family in Lansingburgh, and it is not known exactly what he did in this lingering or malingering in Boston.

The intrepid and imaginative biographer Hershel Parker *wants* him to have visited the sainted Judge Shaw and thereby to have made a closer acquaintance with the fated Elizabeth Shaw, later to become Melville's wife. The biographer has composed quite a number of lively pages about what *must* have gone on in the attractive parlors of the Shaw house on Mount Vernon Street. This enjoyable scene is quite useful as an addition to the scanty evidence about the courtship leading to the marriage that will become a fact three years later. On the other hand, Melville was in a humbled condition, ill dressed, bearded, with little to show for himself except seafaring yarns and a great lump of experience direly unsuitable to the green swards and proud cobbles of Boston. He had sought anonymity, and now once more he was to be a citizen, a Melville and a Gansevoort.

The two families are at least rich in offspring. There are brothers and sisters, cousins, grandchildren, wives and husbands, for scholars to track from birth to death, weddings to be acknowledged, disgraces to make their vivid appearance, letters, like gold coins, to turn up more than a century later—all because of the genius of one. With an obvious fondness for perpetuating the line, the two families give males the same name over and over again. There are four Hermans, five by the name of Allan, four by the name of Thomas. Gansevoort, Herman's older brother, and Allan, his younger brother, were lawyers in New York, and Gansevoort was much in the news when Herman landed back in Boston. Indeed, the brother was a celebrity at the time, a voluble supporter of the Democratic Party. He went about the country speaking to large crowds in New York and in the Middle West. His oratory was flamboyant, lengthy, wildly evangelizing in spirit on behalf of the candidates, first Van Buren and then James Polk; "gas and glory," Horace Greeley described it.

Gansevoort had visited old John Quincy Adams in his last days as president, called on Andrew Jackson in the Hermitage in Tennessee and on Henry Clay in Kentucky. When Polk was elected to the highest office, Gansevoort was off to Washington to receive his reward—a position in the administration. That did not succeed, but he was appointed to the American legation in London, a lucky matter for his brother Herman and for the future of *Typee*.

And at last, back in Lansingburgh, things were somewhat improved, and the writing of *Typee* began and was apparently continued in Manhattan in rooms shared with Herman's younger brother Allan. We read again and again that when the stories of the vagabond years were told, the teller was urged to "write it down." Many have held forth over their schnapps and received a like urging to proceed from the conversation to the blank white page. A day or perhaps only an hour is a brusque education. But Melville from the first had everything at hand—language, narrative gift, ideas about his experience, inspiration—and there he was, his life ahead of him, and the inclination he had shown years before when he sent sketches to the local newspapers and they were published; not much space needed be given to the urgings of young ladies or the family as a spur to composition. And in any case, what he wrote were to be boys' books, if you like, adventures of ambiguous morality and intellectual skepticism.

Melville offered chapters of *Typee* to Harper Brothers, the publisher of Dana's *Two Years Before the Mast,* a popular seagoing story. The book was rejected on the suspicion that it could not be true. A devastating rebuff, but not one of history's famous disreputable denials; the question of the truthfulness haunted the book after successful publication. Perhaps the great mystery about the writing of Melville, in this first book, is his astonishing confidence not only in style but in what you might call his soapbox freedom of opinion about traders, Christianizing invaders, and the arrogant assumption of the inferiority of helpless natives.

The enormities perpetrated in the South Seas upon some inoffensive islanders well-nigh pass belief. These things are seldom proclaimed at home; they happen at the very ends of the earth; they are done in a corner, and there are none to reveal them. But there is, nevertheless, many a petty trader that has navigated the Pacific whose course from island to island might be traced by a series of cold-blooded robberies, kidnappings, and murders, the iniquity of which might be considered almost sufficient to send her guilty timbers to the bottom of the sea.

Gansevoort Melville, soon to be off to his post in London, was visited by a friend, Thomas Nichols, who had dropped into the office to offer congratulations. There he read the incomplete manuscript and advised Gansevoort to offer it to English publishers who, in the common practice at the time, published American authors and offered the works for a reprint publication in the United States.

Gansevoort, always sickly and without long to live, had not left his fervently expressive self back at the political rallies. The American ambassador to England at the time was Louis McLane, a southerner and a properly cautious diplomat. He had not been consulted about President Polk's incendiary appointment and, in addition, came to find Gansevoort's promotion of his own ideas quite irregular and annoying. He tried to have him transferred to Constantinople, but there was no opening.

Meanwhile, Gansevoort had taken the chapters of *Typee* to the publisher John Murray, who was sufficiently interested to ask for more, and when further pages arrived he, not without unspoken reservations, offered a contract. The celebrated Washington Irving, leaving his post as ambassador to Spain, called on his friend Louis McLane, who was away, and instead he met with the sycophantic

Gansevoort. The opportunity to read the early part of *Typee* came about, and Irving was pleased. His own American publisher was based in London, and the manuscript was sent him to consider. The terms for publication in Wiley and Putnam's *Library of Choice Reading* were promptly arranged, and except for troublesome revisions and flagrant excisions, Melville's entrance into the literary world came about with remarkable speed and felicity. He immediately started to write *Omoo*.

Typee was read and widely reviewed. Walt Whitman in the *Brooklyn Eagle:* "A strange, graceful, most readable book this . . . to hold in one's hand and pore dreamily over of a summer day." Margaret Fuller: "With a view to ascertaining the truth, it would be well if the societies, now engaged in providing funds for such enterprises [missionary], would read the particulars, they will find in this book."

Hawthorne reviewed *Typee* in the Salem newspaper:

This book is lightly but vigorously written; and we are acquainted with no work that gives a freer and more effective picture of barbarian life, in that unadulterated state of which there are now so few specimens remaining. The gentleness of disposition that seems akin to the delicious climate, is shown in contrast with the traits of savage fierceness. . . . He has that freedom of view—it would be too harsh to call it laxity of principle—which renders him tolerant of codes of morals that may be little in accordance with our own, a spirit proper enough to a young and adventurous sailor, and which makes his book the more wholesome to our staid landsmen.

Nevertheless, Melville was painfully challenged by the accusations of untruthfulness and by doubts of *Typee*'s authenticity. And then a fortuity rescued him. His friend Toby, Richard Tobias Greene, read about the book and sent a note to the *Buffalo Commercial Advertiser* saying that he survived and could testify to the accuracy of *Typee* for the time he was present.

Melville visited Greene and came away with a portrait and a lock of hair, objects of sentiment and perhaps judiciousness should the nagging press insist he had imagined the resurrected Toby. The resurrected Toby came to be a celebrity in his hometown and the papers were publishing his "own story" as he narrated or wrote it for the local press. It was picked up by other papers and thus threatened to undercut Melville's "sequel" about Toby's affirming account, for which he was demanding extra payment from *Typee*'s publishers. In his version, Melville employs the omniscient narrator of fiction and freely enters Toby's mind in the accounting of his escape and his thwarted intention to rescue Tommo. The telling is apparently valid in the large if somewhat suspicious in the small, the creative detail.

Typee is a fierce work despite the pastoral mode of many scenes. The summery, green and golden island is overlaid with a bleak, primitive, and repetitive rhythm. There is food, sleep, battling with other tribes, and sexual freedom turned rather perfunctory in the absence of or indifference to privacy and other formalities. Toby fled as quickly as possible and intended to take his crippled companion with him. Had Melville been in residence for the claimed four months, the experience does not bear thinking about.

Gansevoort died in London in May 1846. He had lived long enough to know the publication of *Typee* and to try to manage the publisher's revisions and expurgations. The overweaning enthusiasm and attention he gave to his brother's book were in every way significant for its fate. Otherwise, the rejection by Harper Brothers might well have been the end of it. Gansevoort in his youth had often been in poor health; at the time he was seeing Herman off on the *Acushnet,* he was lingering in Boston to solicit a "loan" from Judge Shaw in order to take a cruise with the hope of improving his condition. After a short illness in London, he died in his rooms; there was a small ceremony in Westminster Abbey and the Melvilles petitioned Washington for the return of the body. Grievous times for the family, the eldest son dead at thirty-one, the family pride. And that left Herman and, as it turned out, the mother and sisters to move in with him when he married Elizabeth Shaw.

Typee was dedicated to Lemuel Shaw, chief justice of the Commonwealth of Massachusetts. This noble gentleman had taken on an importunate and improvident tribe when in his youth he had a friendship with Allan, Melville's father, and sought to marry Allan's sister Nancy Melville, who died before the union could take place. The Shaws were a prominent, well-to-do Boston family. No doubt Colonel Robert Shaw, celebrated as the leader of the black 54th Massachusetts Regiment, cruelly annihilated in South Carolina in the Civil War, was a connection, although he is not mentioned by Melville in his war poems. Colonel Shaw was "buried with his niggers," and his haunting statue by Saint-Gaudens stands near the Boston State House.

Elizabeth

WHILE HERMAN WAS AWAY for his four years, Elizabeth Shaw had become a close friend of his sister Helen. The two young women visited back and forth, and Elizabeth was in the house in Lansingburgh when Melville was struggling with the reviews and expurgations of *Typee* and writing *Omoo*. They became engaged, and perhaps the future groom had not the leisure for a provincial courtship. The matter of income, so well known to Judge Shaw in connection with the Melvilles, seemed to have delayed the marriage for a time. Melville went to Washington, with respectable references, in the hope of receiving some sort of government appointment. He did not succeed, and it is not hard to imagine that examiners, with their rich experience in interviewing, could get a whiff of reluctance to succeed in Melville himself.

The marriage with Elizabeth Shaw took place in Boston on August 4, 1847, and they had a honeymoon in the White Mountains of New Hampshire, Montreal, and Quebec. He was twenty-eight years old, and she was twenty-five. It was a dynastic marriage of Melville, Gansevoort, and Shaw, Eastern seaboard aristocracy at least of birth and early emigration; a few heirlooms in the closet.

Melville had a measure of public distinction with *Typee* and *Omoo*–property of a kind. Not known then, not even by himself, was the frantic application ahead, the fearsome embarkation on a creative life, the unromantic presentation by workers in all the arts of objects for which there is seldom a specific public need.

In any case, Melville was self-propelled and at home surrounded by a puzzled sympathy. The feeling of the family, of his wife, about individual books is a blank, a condition perhaps to be preferred to a household raging at critics, publishers, and booksellers and inducing paranoid excitements.

Elizabeth Shaw was what would be called a "very nice young woman." She was good-natured, friendly, and well brought up by her indulgent father and by an agreeable stepmother, her own mother having died at her birth. She raised four children, endured the tragedy of the death of two, put up with her troublesome mother-in-law and the long years of her husband's intense inner life and creative pain and disappointment. She copied his manuscripts in the manner of the Countess Tolstoy, but did not, so far as we know, express the raging egotism and demand for attention that drove Tolstoy to escape to the train station and there to die. Lizzie Melville was not as brilliant as the Countess and did not have to endure obsequious disciples and flatterers, although for Herman a young male amanuensis or literary admirer might have been pleasing–as they were for Tolstoy.

In *The Kreutzer Sonata,* Tolstoy would write of marriage as "two convicts serving a life sentence of hard labor welded to the same chain," which led the Countess to threaten to jump into the pond. As Elizabeth Shaw labored on a weary evening to bring the skewered, cramped handwriting to legibility, she could read of "the disenchanting glasses of matrimonial days and nights." Well, pass on in the manner of a court stenographer clicking away about heads severed with a hatchet.

On the other hand, Tolstoy wrote of young love with great beauty and sympathy, while the accent in Melville is on the soul love of Jonathan and David. And what did the burdened wife think of the incestuous follies of *Pierre* and about a light magazine piece, "I and My Chimney," in which a husband is trying to save a treasured bit of household familiarity and the wife is in a rampaging renovation mood? Elizabeth would say that the obstructing female virago was his mother, not herself. Otherwise, the strain voiced was in the matter of Melville's health, his bad eyes, his bad back, his sciatica, his gruesome overwork.

The marriage was more prudent for Melville than for his wife. He might long for male friendship, even for love, but marriage changed him from an unanchored wanderer into an obsessive writer, almost as if there, in a house, in a neighborhood, there was nothing else for this man to do except to use the capital he had found in himself with the writing of *Typee* and *Omoo*. And, of course, Melville that he was, sharing the family denial of the economics of life, his children would not be sent out to sell candles so long as there was a Gansevoort in Albany and Judge Shaw in Boston to hear their cries.

After twenty years of her husband's frenzy, his bad

temper with too much to drink at night, Lizzie seriously considered a separation. It was thought quite in order, even urgent, by her half brother Sam Shaw and by the clergyman she consulted. She could not at last take the step, although the dilemma this faithful and conventional wife faced must have been greatly alarming. They endured to the end; forty-four years of marriage it was.

Omoo, Mardi

OMOO: It's away from the cannibal paradise as he manages to board the *Lucy Ann,* a wreck, "a small, slatternly looking craft, her hulls and spars a dingy black, rigging all slack and bleached nearly white." And yet the Australian whaler, called the *Julia,* or "little Jule," in the book, was, beneath her tattered rags, a lithe dancing maiden: "Blow high or blow low, she was always ready for the breeze; and when she dashed the waves from her prow, and pranced, and pawed the sea, you never thought of her patched sails and blistered hull." This affectionate lyric to an abused boat shines in comparison to the disorderly and careless riffraff who command her fate. And Melville himself is not in good shape; he is bearded, hair flowing, wrapped in native cloth, but once afloat seeking among the drunken, venereal crew someone to talk to.

Captain Guy, the commander, is not one of the usual pipe-smoking tyrants, but an original being. He is "no more suited to sea-going than a hair-dresser." In one amazing scene, we find the Captain coming from his quarters to investigate the noise of a fight. He who will be Melville's companion, called Doctor Long Ghost, cries out in a "camp" aside, "Ah! Miss Guy, is that you? Now, my dear, go right home, or you'll get hurt." Captain Guy is quite ill and will leave the boat, giving over command to the vicious, hotheaded, drunken mate named Jermin.

Long Ghost had been the ship's surgeon and enjoyed privileges, such as drinking and playing cards with the captain. In an argument about politics the doctor had knocked the captain down, been disciplined, and escaped; when he was returned to the ship, he abandoned his more lofty position and chose to live with the ordinary seamen. Long Ghost enjoys one of Melville's portraits:

> He was over six feet high—a tower of bones, with a complexion absolutely colorless, fair hair, and a light, unscrupulous gray eye, twinkling occasionally with the very devil of mischief. . . . And from whatever high estate Doctor Long Ghost may have fallen, he had certainly at some time or other spent money, drunk Burgundy, and associated with gentlemen. . . . As for his learning, he quoted Virgil, and talked of Hobbes of Malmsbury, besides repeating poetry by the canto, especially *Hudibras*. He was, moreover, a man who had seen the world. . . . he could refer to an amour he had in Palermo, and the quality of coffee to be drunk in Muscat.

The mate Jermin: "a face deeply pitted with the smallpox." For the rest, there was a fierce little squint out of one eye; the nose had a rakish twist to one side; while his large mouth, and great white teeth, looked "absolutely sharkish when he laughed." Jermin's drunken command of the *Ju-*

lia when the sick captain is taken off the ship arouses the crew to mutiny, which is joined by Melville and Long Ghost. The French frigate *La Reine Blanche* was in the port of Papeete and arrested the mutineers and held them in the brig for several days. From there, they were held by the British in an outdoor jail, whose warden was a relaxed person named Uncle Bob.

A good deal of the mutiny action and jailing has the feeling of a Gilbert and Sullivan operetta. Note the English consul Wilson conducting an inquiry:

> "I want no *buts,*" cried the consul, breaking in: "answer me *yes* or *no*–have you anything to say against Mr. Jermin?"
>
> "I was going to say, sir; Mr. Jermin's a very good man, but then–"
>
> "So much then for that part of the business," exclaimed Wilson smartly, "you have nothing to say against him, I see."

Omoo is scattered geographically, unlike the claustrophobic beauty of the island in *Typee*. Indeed, there is a superfluity of incident, a crowded chorus of characters that will include an American, Zeke, and his partner, Shorty, who are farming yams on the island; native dinner parties, Queen Pomaree and family, a church service and an extraordinary sermon preached in "The Church of the Cocoa-Nuts," a Polynesian adaptation of Christianity. There is rough competition between the French Catholics and the English Protestants, and Melville is entirely unmoved by their efforts and indifferent to the critics of *Typee* in the matter of religious proselytizing.

> In fact, there is, perhaps, no race upon earth, less disposed, by nature, to the admonitions of Christianity, than the people of the South Sea. And this assertion is made with full knowledge of what is called the "Great Revival at the Sandwich Islands," about the year 1836; when several thousands were in the course of a few weeks, admitted into the bosom of the Church. . . . Added to all this, is a quality inherent in Polynesians, and more akin to hypocrisy than anything else. It leads them to assume the most passionate interest, in matters for which they feel little or none whatsoever, but in which, those whose power they dread, or whose favor they court, they believe to be at all affected.

Omoo was published in England on March 30, 1847, and in the United States the following month, just a few weeks before his marriage to Elizabeth Shaw. The book was widely reviewed, attention given to the comparison between the new effort and *Typee,* alarm about the disrespect for missionaries trying to bring the ordeal and triumph of Jesus to the unsanctified. Melville is married and moving to Manhattan to a house on Fourth Avenue, just a block or so from downtown Fifth Avenue. He leased the house with his brother Allan, newly married, and into it moved his mother and four sisters, making seven Melvilles and two wives.

D. H. Lawrence, writing later about *Typee* and *Omoo,*
has this to say about the newly settled family man:

> Melville came home to face out the long rest of his life.
> He married and had an ecstasy of a courtship and fifty
> years of disillusion. He had just furnished his home with
> disillusions. No more Typees. No more paradises. No
> more Fayaways. A mother: a gorgon. A home: a torture
> box. A wife: a thing with clay feet. Life: a sort of dis-
> grace. . . . The whole shameful business just making a
> man writhe. Melville writhed for eighty years.

Lawrence gives more years of writhing than Melville
was allowed, since he died at the age of seventy-two and in
this reading not a moment too soon. Still, there is *something*
to be said for Lawrence's wild freedom as a critic and as a
reader sensing the blank page of Melville's emotional life,
even his social life so essentially friendless. Melville didn't
want to be known; he is one who treasures, insists on
anonymity.

Think of Dana's *Two Years Before the Mast:* His "I" is
everywhere present, telling us who he is: a Bostonian,
longing to return safely to Cambridge; one who has studied Latin and French but had to learn Spanish to make the
overdressed Spanish settlers in California come alive on
the page. He appears a "normal" young man, usually
cheerful or wishing to be; as alert as Melville to the horror
of an innately sadistic captain flogging a helpless seaman
just for the top mariner's right to do so. But Dana is

always there in his own everyday person, one who has dropped out of Harvard but will go back at the end of the journey.

Melville's "I" is an observer, a narrator, who takes part in the action when it is necessary, but except for pages of *Redburn,* where he appears, and disguised even there, he is never asked who he is, where he comes from, even though he, without a biography, is keen to create the background of many on shipboard. Melville writes fiercely, anxiously, tirelessly—that's all of his life; even in the years of "withdrawal" he does what he can after the days at the Custom House. He is in love with language, with reading, thinking; he travels when he can, to get away. We can wonder if he knew his own stormy genius. In America, then, the idea of being an "artist," one of peculiar endowment and privilege, did occur to some, certainly to Whitman, but perhaps not to Melville who lived it out, almost helplessly, it seems.

With *Typee* and *Omoo,* Melville was a known writer. In New York, his editor for *Typee* was Evert Duyckinck, very much a popular figure and bon vivant, who subsequently became editor of *Literary World,* an important magazine at the time. Edgar Allan Poe, in his incomparable portraits of mostly forgotten authors and publishing fixtures, writes of Duyckinck:

He is about five feet eight inches high, somewhat slender. The forehead, phrenologically, is a good one; eyes and hair light; the whole expression of the face that of serenity and benevolence, contributing to give an idea of youthfulness. He is probably thirty, but does not seem to be twenty-five. His dress, also, is in full keeping with his character, scrupulously neat but plain, and conveying an instantaneous conviction of the gentleman. He is a descendant of one of the oldest and best Dutch families in the state. Married.

This little sketch by Poe in "The Literati of New York City" does not give the flavor of his slyly brash collision with the poets, male and female, the novelists of both sexes, the reciters, the editors, the married and the unmarried, the attractive and "the person about whom there is nothing especially to be noted." He takes note of "Sarah Margaret Fuller" and thinks her book on women in the nineteenth century belongs in "Curiosities of American Literature." He praises her review of Longfellow in *The Dial* and on the subject of Longfellow adds: "The country is disgraced by the evident toadyism which would reward to his social position and influence, to his fine paper and large type, to his morocco bindings and gilt edges, to his flattering portrait of himself . . . that amount of indiscriminate approbation which neither could nor would have been given to the poems themselves."

Melville did not meet Poe, but it is known that he read his poems and his tales. With the convivial Duyckinck some "literary evenings" were spent, popular authors of the day were met, theatricals attended. The Astor Place riots took place near Melville's house, and a curious New York scene it was. The English actor William Macready was appearing in *Macbeth,* and this was somehow thought to be an insult to the local celebrity of Shakespeare, Edwin Forrest. Gangs like the Plug-Uglies and Dead Rabbits mounted a patriotic assault on the theater, throwing stones, breaking windows, forcing Macready to make his escape with the help of John Jacob Astor and Washington Irving. At a subsequent performance, the rioters stormed again and were met with three hundred policemen and two hundred state militia. They fired into the crowd, killing almost two dozen of the rebels. At the time, it was noted that among those signing a petition to allow Macready to appear and go through his classical paces was Herman Melville.

Mardi, a perturbation. Melville did not leave the sea for this work that in 1849 followed *Typee* and *Omoo* but veered away from the documentation of four years in the Pacific and did not return until *White-Jacket.* It appears that he somehow wanted to honor the mind and spirit, the flight of his vision that had soared beyond the autobiographical mode of jumping from one ship to another, landing here and there, and offering the narration more or less as truthful. Leslie Fiedler calls *Mardi* a "honeymoon book," and perhaps it was a trip signifying a move from one state to another.

The book starts on a whaling vessel, the *Arcturion,* but it is a retrograde boat, hunting not the pugnacious sperm whale but the "sullen, inert" right whale. The captain in an offhand remark says he, the writer, might leave "if he can." So he jumps ship in an open boat and, as always, with a companion. This is to be Jarl, from the island of Skye,

Viking blood in him. From some "unguarded allusions to Belles-Lettres," Jarl showed proper, if illiterate, respect for the "I" as a special one to be a sailor.

The early pages of *Mardi* are, like plums in a pie, filled with illustrious names: Spinoza, Kant, Luther, Rabelais, Buffon, Sir Thomas Browne, "who, while exploding 'vulgar Errors,' heartily hugged all the mysteries of the Pentateuch"; Wouwermans, "who once painted a bull bait"; and Claude's "setting summer suns." The prevailing tone is attractive in a jocular fashion and also jocular in a sentimental mood. If Melville had not cared so greatly about the fiction, we might have thought it a long, long *jeu d'espirt*. *Mardi* is the same length as *Moby-Dick,* if not some few pages longer.

The open boat comes ashore on many fantastical islands, and the narrator is transmogrified into Taji, the sun god awaited by the credulous natives. Along the way, Taji will rescue Yillah, a white-skinned princess with golden hair, and they enter a bower of bliss until Yillah vanishes, never to be found again, suggesting that the beautiful beloved is only a phantom. The action is interrupted by many *recitatives* about legends and the island's imaginative histories. "A story! Hear him: the solemn philosopher is desirous of regaling us with a tale! But, pray begin."

Among the reviews collected by Hershel Parker, the inclination to follow Melville's unanchored poetical prose is often hard to resist: "Come back, O Herman, from thy cloudy supermundane flight." That sort of thing. The failure of *Mardi* was apparently not expected by the author, who, as the professional he had now become, thought to

offer the public a respite from his previous youthful journeys and to use his own accumulating powers of prose
composition and imagination.

It is difficult to figure out just how Melville's books
were written, how long each took, since they come out
headfirst like multiple births, one after another. *Redburn*
was published five months after *Mardi* and *White-Jacket* six
months later. During 1849 he took a four-month trip to
London and the Continent, and his first son, Malcolm,
was born one month before *Mardi* and two before *Redburn*.
A fertile span indeed.

In London, Melville was a visiting writer of note, meeting his publishers, dining out with the firm's stars, touring
every museum and cathedral, buying books; and then he
proceeded to Paris, Bruges, Brussels, Cologne—a sort of
Grand Tour by a very eager student. *White-Jacket* was published in London while he was there and came out a
month later in New York. The subtitle of the book is *The
World in a Man-of-War*. After some months on another whaling ship, the note to *White-Jacket* reads: "In the year 1843 I
shipped as an 'ordinary seaman' on board of a United
States frigate, then lying in a harbor on the Pacific Ocean.
After remaining in this frigate for more than a year, I was
discharged from the service upon the vessel's arrival
home. My man-of-war experiences and observations are
incorporated in the present volume."

White-Jacket was apparently composed with Melville's
usual speed and his startling command of narration, here
largely given to the structure and practice of the U.S.
Navy. The white jacket is a sort of joke and a wearisome

one. Instead of the usual pea jacket, the narrator is on board with a thick jacket of white duck for warmth, and the garment does not seem to be symbolic of anything beyond a willed maladaptation to the demands of a man-of-war. The ship, except for the pretensions of the Commodore and the staff, is more pleasant than a whaler; there is a library, a crew congenial for the most part, a cast of characters roaming about in the exposition. One, a little fellow who writes poetry; another, named Selvagee: "With all the intrepid effeminacy of your true dandy, he still continued his Cologne-water baths, and sported his lace-bordered handkerchiefs in the very teeth of a tempest."

And there is the friendship with a genuine person, Jack Chase, to whom *Billy Budd* will be dedicated. "He was a Briton and a true blue; tall and well-knit, with a clear open eye"; a gentleman, courteous, well-read, who could recite parts of the great Portuguese epic poem *Lusiads* by Camoëns, in the original language. "Jack drinks, but otherwise he is a free spirit, strong and yet fair-minded, a warrior for the 'rights of man.'"

The most compelling scenes in the book are the pages that tell of bestial floggings. *"All hands witness punishment, ahoy!"* and this is exact; all must be on hand, as if in participation of the ordained ritual. The first flogging is of six crewmen, one after another, each accused of fighting about a trivial matter. Sometimes when the object of punishment seems near death before the required lashes have been completed, he is sent away to rest and, when recovered, brought back for the remaining strokes. Melville will propose his own Articles of War:

Irrespective of incidental considerations, we assert that flogging in the navy is opposed to the essential dignity of man, which no legislator has a right to violate; that it is oppressive, and glaringly unequal in its operations; that it is utterly repugnant to the spirit of our democratic institutions; indeed that it involves a lingering trait of the worst times of a barbarous feudal aristocracy; in a word, we denounce it as religiously, morally and immutably *wrong.*

The year 1850: Melville has taken his family to Pittsfield, the farm bought by the grandfather and now mismanaged by Robert, the feckless son of the errant Uncle Tom. Here in the summery vacation, amid many other tagalong Melvilles, babies, and visitors, somehow Herman will proceed from *White-Jacket* to *Moby-Dick.* A daunting immersion in unexplored waters; there's that facile thought and the wonder why he went on, sunk in debt as he was, landlocked and soon to assume Arrowhead with shadowy funds. The conditions Melville is long accustomed to as his second skin: everlasting bankruptcy and everlasting composition. The pages sent off to reluctant addresses and the next book begun.

There, in the Massachusetts countryside, he will meet Hawthorne and go home to write, anonymously, a review of *Mosses from an Old Manse,* to be published in *Literary World.* It is not a close reading of the stories but an exalted appreciation of Hawthorne's mood, his "blackness," his melancholy view of man's fate, his misappropriation by the public as a smiling, sunny writer. A statement of principle: the *Power of Blackness,* Hawthorne's and, of course, Melville's.

Whether Hawthorne has simply availed himself of this mystical blackness as a means of the wondrous effects he makes to produce his lights and shades; or whether there really lurks in him, perhaps unknown to himself, a touch of Puritanic gloom—this, I cannot altogether tell. Certain it is, however, that this power of blackness in him derives its appeal to that Calvinistic sense of Innate Depravity and Original Sin, from whose visitations, in some shape or another, no deeply thinking mind is always and wholly freed.

"I feel that this Hawthorne has dropped germinous seeds into my soul." Hawthorne and Melville met in the Berkshires, and a friendship developed unique in Melville's life, unique in inspiration and in disappointment. The Hawthornes would learn that Melville was the author of the anonymous review, "the shock of recognition" of one writer for another. On the other hand, Hawthorne had written one of the most interesting notes on *Typee,* and so there existed a certain reciprocity of literary favors and appreciation. The Hawthorne household was much more placid than the Melville: there was a measure of uxoriousness in the nature of husband Nathaniel that husband Herman did not seem to share. However, Sophia Hawthorne was, in her letters, quite approving of the young admirer. He was invited to spend several nights in the household, a permission not often granted.

Moby-Dick was dedicated to Hawthorne, who wrote the publisher favorably about it, even protesting a notice in the *Literary World* that was especially irksome to Melville. He did not review the book but wrote a last letter that ignited the younger man's spirit to a flaming declaration:

> A sense of unspeakable security is in me at this moment, on account of your having understood the book. I have written a wicked book and feel spotless as a lamb. . . . Whence come you Hawthorne? By what right do you drink from my flagon of life? And when I put it to my lips they are yours, not mine. I feel that the Godhead is broken up like the bread at the Supper, and that we are the pieces. Hence this infinite fraternity of feeling.

Melville had found in Hawthorne the lone intellectual and creative friendship of his life, had found another struck by the terror and the dark indifference of the universe. This intensity of reverence, of alliance, could not be returned—for that Hawthorne had Sophia Peabody. Melville's emotions were not indiscreet; he was animated by a need for a mirror reflecting his own struggle to honor his vision, his experience in the battle with words, images, paragraphs, structure, pages and pages. He would share the fate of being a writer in America, share his ragged banner: Failure is the test of greatness. But there was a disjunction of temperament, an inequality of fervor.

Hawthorne is in every way a more plausible man and citizen than Melville, who has about him, even in settled married life, much of the renegade, the scars of knowing, choosing, the bleak underside of life. When Melville sailed on the *Acushnet,* Hawthorne was long out of Bowdoin College in Maine, where his classmates were Longfellow and Franklin Pierce, later President of the United States. Melville's mates were drunken, venereal, negligent, brutalized wastrels one would hurry past on the street. We note that Hawthorne would hold the position of Consul in Liverpool but that his previous recommendation for a similar post for Melville came to nothing. Apparently Melville did not appear to be quite suitable.

When Melville met Hawthorne he was in his garments as a gentleman and had done most of his work, even the beginning of *Moby-Dick.* But he is needy as an orphan, and Pittsfield was not a shipboard. The relations between the two men were creditable to both, but a younger, yearning writer was somehow intrusive, too much *there,* not in personal attendance but in spiritual identification. "Opulent in withheld replies," a phrase from the long Melville poem, *Clarel,* might, in F. O. Matthiessen's view, express Melville's late feelings about Hawthorne.

Moby-Dick

"*CALL ME ISHMAEL*": the three words a resonant, epical invocation of *Moby-Dick,* an unexpected masterpiece written by the harassed scribe. Ishmael and Ahab: a naming so blunt and fitting and adhering it alone can seem to be the root of the inspiration that seized or engulfed Melville. Single names they are and neither promising in association for male children who, instead, begin their lives under the protective and paternal hope of Abraham, Moses, Joseph, or Noah.

Ishmael, a "wild man" sired by Abraham and born to the serving maid Hagar with the wily connivance of the aged, barren Sarah. A quite modern little playlet it is in the Scriptures. Hagar going about the house with her little man-child Ishmael, sired by the overwhelming Abraham, became in her fertile honor assuming and condescending to her mistress, the matriarch, who did not receive it in silence and forbearance. Divine intervention was sought for the condition of Sarah, "well-stricken in age," and in a neat turn of Biblical phrasing, "it had ceased to be with Sarah after the manner of women." So, Isaac, the heir to Abraham's riches and the special covenant with God, is born, and Sarah takes her revenge by a wifely mistreatment of

Hagar, who flees the house with her child Ishmael. Abraham, the primeval begetter, assumes responsibility for the bastard offspring, for his care and costs; the child is circumcised and sent on his destiny, which is to marry an Egyptian and to be the "father," as it were, of Bedouin tribes.

Ishmael, the narrator of *Moby-Dick* in the first person, is the creative intelligence of the novel. Melville himself, as a sailor in real life, was perforce a wild man wandering in the wilderness of the Atlantic and the Pacific. Perhaps he chose the name with an ironical amusement as he sat writing at his desk in the Berkshires amidst the fields and trees. Or perhaps not.

Ahab, one of the kings of Israel, takes the wicked Jezebel as his wife, worships the heathen god Baal, and comes to a bad end. Melville's Ahab has lost his leg in a battle with the white whale called Moby Dick. His life, his soul, is overwhelmed by an obsession to search the seas in vengeance for his terrible wounding. In this way, Ahab can be seen to have fallen into idolatry, an unwholesome worship of the claims of his private destiny, a blasphemous disregard of nature, the seas, and the creatures within it; an agnostic disowning of his fellow beings, the crew who will perish with him. But *Moby-Dick* is a fiction, and Ahab is a shaggy old sea warrior from Nantucket created out of a broad, devouring conception, yes, but also touched by homely sufferings and losses, all to be expressed in a rhetoric of beauty and extremity.

Moby-Dick was published in 1851 when Melville was thirty-two years old: *only* thirty-two, with five novels behind him, some early success and more failure, with a wife, a son, and another to be born four days after the appearance of the English edition. Trees and fields and debts. Another sea story, this time an immensity of aspiration that makes the previous tales seem to be boys' books. There is the old ferocity of the occupation that sets the predators, the whaling men, against the powerful monarch of the sea. Here the whale is a being with a name, a history: Ahab's harpoons "lie all twisted and wrenched in him," and for that Ahab has surrendered a leg. A fratricidal battle it is, with the whale personified by its whiteness, its having a name, its singularity in the history of Ahab, who has in his forty years at sea killed many whales and yet has made Moby Dick his enemy in a hatred to the death.

The daunting narrative begins plainly enough and cheerfully with Ishmael on the streets of Manhattan, the metropolis with its two rivers. Even the tame waters of the city cause the citizens to stand on the banks idly dreaming due to the powerful stir to the imagination that arises from the waters of the earth. "We see ourselves in all rivers and oceans. It is the image of the ungraspable phantoms of life, and this is the key to it all." Ishmael, a young New Yorker, has decided to go to sea on a whale ship, drawn by "the overwhelming idea of the great whale himself. Such a portentous and mysterious monster roused all my curiosity." And here in the opening reverie is a hint of what is to come.

> The great flood gates of the wonder-world swing open, and in the wild conceits that swayed me to my purpose, two and two there floated in my inmost soul, endless

processions of the whale, and midmost of them all, one grand hooded phantom, like a snow hill in the air.

So Ishmael is off to the Massachusetts ports of New Bedford and Nantucket, where he will join the *Pequod,* Captain Ahab, and all the others in the maelstrom, the mania, the pitiless search, the calm days and the menacing energy of a typhoon, and at last, the perfervid gladiators, the Whale and the Captain, in unappeasable fury, "carried the smallest chip of the *Pequod* out of sight." The roiling sea is beyond, but it was Melville's genius to introduce the wildly peopled, digressive, epic tale with the cobbled streets of New Bedford and Nantucket and Ishmael's nights at the Spouter-Inn, boyish and baffling as they are. For want of a separate accommodation he is to bed down with a harpooner named Queequeg, whose entrance is dramatically prolonged for "effect."

Appear he does: a huge apparition tattooed from head to foot. "There was no hair on his head—none to speak of at least—nothing but a small scalp-knot twisted upon his forehead. His bald purplish head now looked for all the world like a mildewed skull. . . .

"Upon waking next morning about daylight, I found Queequeg's arm thrown over me in the most loving and affectionate manner. You had almost thought I had been his wife." Another night before they make their way from New Bedford to Nantucket.

How it is I know not; but there is no place like a bed for confidential disclosures between friends. Man and wife, they say, there open the very bottom of their souls to each other, and some old couples lie and chat over old times till nearly morning. Thus, then in our hearts' honeymoon, lay I and Queequeg—a cozy, loving pair.

Innocence in the implication, our implication, more than a hundred years later; innocence in the imagination? The warm bed in the Spouter-Inn, the young Ishmael and the outrageously defaced "cannibal"? A pastoral, somehow tropical lyric, a paean to comradeship, perhaps. As the narrative proceeds, the unquestioning or innocent erotic lyricism takes a turn of fantastical brilliance, a wild, sunlit flow of adjective; an active, sonorous explosion of sheer sensation arising from the effluent sperm of the great sea creature.

The *Pequod* is at sea; a sperm whale has been captured, eviscerated, and the sperm drained for commercial use into tubs on the deck. Certain lumps that will be formed are to be squeezed to unite them with the liquid. Ishmael, "I," tells of the unique pleasure of his hands in the vat squeezing the lumps.

Squeeze! Squeeze! Squeeze! all the morning long. I squeezed that sperm till I myself almost melted into it; I squeezed that sperm till a strange sort of insanity came over me; and I found myself unwittingly squeezing my co-laborers hands in it. . . . Come; let us squeeze hands all around; nay, let us all squeeze ourselves into each other; let us squeeze ourselves universally into the very milk and sperm of kindness.

Back to the opening pages of *Moby-Dick,* pages of a strong structural felicity as a balance to the boundless voyage, the monologues, the encyclopedic insertion of the shape of the whaling ship, the whale species, the instruments available at the time, and ever there the plot of an inventive magnitude.* On the Massachusetts streets, imaginative clouds of premonition, the shadows of the bewildering structure of the destination of Captain Ahab himself.

The connubial nights in New Bedford are interrupted by a Sunday-morning visit to the Whaleman's Chapel and to the sermon by Father Mapple. The chapel is the repository of heart-breaking tablets "sacred to the memory of men lost overboard"; to a Captain Hardy "killed by a sperm whale on the coast of Japan"; a plaque in memory of six crewmen "towed out of sight by a whale," the memorial dedicated by their surviving shipmates. Here Melville, in a hortatory reflection common throughout his work, ponders the practice of sacramental grief for the dead who are claimed by religion to be lifted from the watery grave to an eternity of "unspeakable bliss." "But Faith, like a jackal, feeds among the tombs, and even from these dead doubts she gathers her most vital hope."

---

*The distinguished critic R. P. Blackmur would dispute a commendation for Melville as here a master of the art of fiction. He does not see a sufficient education or an inclination to the craft of a "natural" novelist. "Technical defects" and "an inefficient relation between the writer and the formal elements of his medium." *The Lion and the Honeycomb* (Harcourt, Brace, 1965).

Father Mapple has fashioned his church like a ship and by means of a rope ladder mounts the pulpit as though it were a mainmast. He urges the communicants to gather close together: "Starboard gangway, there! Side away to the larboard!" and in this marine transformation he begins his unanchored, incomparable oration on Jonah. The old Biblical miscreant is seen as a common prevaricator, a shady lout such as could be met skulking around any port. As he comes to board the ship, the crew speculates that he's a robber or a bigamist or one of the "missing murderers from Sodom." The captain, suspicious also, takes Jonah aboard because he's a paying passenger. Father Mapple: "Now, Jonah's Captain, shipmates, was one whose discernment detects crime in any, but whose cupidity exposes it only in the penniless. In this world, shipmates, sin that pays its way can travel freely, and without a passport; whereas Virtue, if a pauper, is stopped at all frontiers."

A misbegotten Jonah, redeemed and vomited up from the churning stomach of the whale by a forgiving God when he admits his sinful ways, is a common Christian view. But the grandeur of the eloquence of the old whaler-preacher, Father Mapple, comes from the dark knowledge of the debased and debasing life of the pursuers and killers of the whale.

In Nantucket, ready to meet the *Pequod,* Ishmael and Queequeg are followed by a forbidding, chattering old sailor who goes by the name of Elijah, the Biblical scourge of the Biblical Ahab. In an antic, pestering intrusion of "diabolical incoherence," Elijah suggests bad luck or worse for the voyage. "Good bye to ye. Shan't see ye again very soon, I guess; unless it's before the Grand Jury."

Again, as preparation for Ahab, who does not actually appear until the ship has been under sail for some days, there is an artful foreshadowing. Two old whalers, now shore pilots and former shipmates of Ahab, in an interview with Ishmael and Queequeg about the matter of their suitability as crew, show Ahab to be a descriptive challenge to ordinary men when confronting a human conundrum:

"He ain't sick and he ain't well."

"A grand, ungodly, god-like man."

"Ahab's above the common; Ahab's been to college, as well as 'mong the cannibals."

"I know, too, that ever since he lost his leg last voyage by that accursed whale, he's been kind of moody–desperate moody and savage sometimes."

"Wrong not Captain Ahab, because he happens to have a wicked name. Besides, my boy, he has a wife–not three voyages wedded–a sweet, resigned girl. Think of that; by that sweet girl that old man had a child."

"No, no, my lad; stricken, blasted, if he be, Ahab has humanities."

The *Pequod* and its vagarious Captain emerge in a suspenseful mist. A leg lost to a whale, but not yet a White Whale named Moby Dick. Scholarship has unearthed the source of the name: "Mocha Dick: or the White Whale of the Pacific" by J. N. Reynolds, published in *Knickerbocker* magazine in 1839, which cites the White Whale as having, in seaman's lore, prodigious strength, a malicious determination to avenge himself and his kind against the harpoons and the ships carrying them.

For the actual destruction of the *Pequod* by Moby Dick, the *Narrative of the Most Extraordinary and Distressing Shipwreck of the Whale-Ship Essex* by Owen Chase (1821), a gruesome reality, a whale-stoved ship, entered Melville's imagination to be transformed by prodigious, fearsome language and by Ahab, who has no ancestor in literature other than all of literature.

The crew of the *Pequod:* Malays, Parsees, Africans; "They were nearly all Islanders on the *Pequod.* . . . *Isolatos* too, I call such, not acknowledging the continent of men, but each *isolato* living on a separate continent of his own." The officers are white Americans, New Englanders, and of these the first mate, Starbuck, is the most vividly, painfully human, the one whose destruction is in the end most searing. A native of Nantucket and a Quaker by descent, Starbuck is thirty years old, with a young wife and child. There he stands, next in line of authority to Ahab, his reason and experience a torture, for he is standing and waiting for a doom foreseen. Ahab will have the doom, he demands it as the expression of himself, what he is, what his will has embraced, and the will fills him with a strange contemplative energy. Starbuck's wrenching helplessness is a suffering of a natural degree different from that of Ahab's wounded body. Ahab is the Captain, and as the captain he can practice barbarous nautical deceits such as breaking the quadrant, which is leading the men to port and not in the direction, away from safety, that Ahab believes the White Whale to be following:

Starbuck:

He had no fancy for lowering for whales after sun-down; for persisting in fighting a fish that too much persisted in fighting him. For, thought Starbuck, I am here in this critical ocean to kill whales for my living, and not to be killed by them for theirs; and that hundreds of men had been so killed Starbuck well knew. What doom was his own father's? Where, in the bottomless deeps, could he find the torn limbs of his brother?

On the deck, Ahab exhorting the men to seek and find the White Whale with the flamboyant intensity of his own crusade and Starbuck: "Vengeance on a dumb brute that simply smote thee from the blindest instinct! Madness! To be enraged with a dumb thing, Captain Ahab, seems blasphemous." The clarity of Starbuck is the measure of his misery, the annihilating paralysis in the prison of the ship, the pity for the distraught old captain, *his captain,* the supremacy of the sea and the fragility of the ships bound upon mastering it, the primitive daring of the whale hunters by which they earn their contempt for the voyagers in the merchant service. Starbuck's loneliness is the conscience remaining in him of the claims of a civilian order, different from the structured autocracy of ocean vessels. The claim of life over Ahab's excited plunge into a metaphysical death that is a true death.*

In a profoundly moving chapter called "The Musket," Starbuck experiences a preternatural testing of his spirit, a testing of his haunted reason as the action proceeds on its disastrous course. A severe typhoon and then a lull. Starbuck goes below to inform the Captain that the danger seems to have abated and it is "fair" on deck. Outside the door, he sees the loaded muskets in the rack. "Starbuck was an honest, upright man, but out of Starbuck's heart, at that instant when he saw the muskets, there strangely evolved an evil thought; . . ."

"He would have shot me once," he murmured, "yes, there's the very musket that he pointed at me; . . . "

But shall this crazed old man be tamely suffered to drag a whole ship's company down to doom with him?–Yes, it would make him the wilful murderer of thirty men or more, if this ship comes to any deadly harm; and come to deadly harm, my soul swears the ship will, if Ahab has his way. If, then, he were this instant–put aside, that crime would not be his.

*Newton Arvin's chapter on "The Whale" is a poetic, majestic immersion that rivals the raging inspiration of Melville himself. His notion of Starbuck is at variance with that expressed here. About Ahab's hubris he writes, "The true antithesis of Hubris is moderation, and moderation is not a cardinal virtue in Melville's calendar; Starbuck embodies that, and Starbuck hovers between a golden *mediocritas* and plain mediocrity."

Ahab is sleeping, and Starbuck is unable to imagine the deed and instead tries to imagine putting the old man in chains, making him a prisoner to be taken home.

What! Hope to wrest this old man's living power from his own living hands? Only a fool would try it. Say he were pinioned even; knotted all over with ropes and hawsers; chained down to ring-bolts on this cabin floor; he would be more hideous than a caged tiger, then. I could not endure the sight; could not possibly fly his howlings; all comfort, sleep itself, inestimable reason would leave me on the long intolerable voyage.

With exact dramatic balance, Melville ends this brilliant Hamlet-like moment with a falling cadence. Starbuck "placed the death-tube in its rack, and left the place."

Ahab, shrewd still despite the sovereignty of blood lust for the white whale, understands the easy excitability of the crew and their impetuous alliance with him in the search. However, passions wane, and "all sailors of all sorts are more or less capricious and unreliable." With this thought he has decided to post a gold Ecuadorian doubloon for "whosoever of ye raises me a white-headed whale, with a wrinkled brow and a crooked jaw; whosoever of ye raises me that white-headed whale, with three holes punctured in his starboard fluke—look ye, whosoever of ye raises me the same white whale, he shall have this gold ounce, my boys!" In his "surmises" Ahab has observed or decided that the permanent constitutional condition of man is "sordidness." Thus the spur, the lottery hope represented by the doubloon.

About Starbuck, Ahab's surmises are otherwise:

> He knew, for example, that however magnetic his ascendancy in some respects was over Starbuck, yet that ascendancy did not cover the complete spiritual man any more than mere corporeal superiority involves intellectual mastership. . . . Starbuck's body and Starbuck's coerced will were Ahab's, so long as Ahab kept his magnet at Starbuck's brain; still he knew that for all this the chief mate, in his soul, abhorred the Captain's quest, and could he, would joyfully disintegrate himself from it, or even frustrate it.

The necessity to the narrative of Starbuck's painful distance from the turbulent and implacable Ahab imperative is a mark of Melville's supreme control of this astounding fiction. But of course it is Ahab's tale; Ahab's and Moby Dick's gladiatorial, hand-to-hand battle, a heathenish defiance.

Ahab: nothing to stand with him in our literature before or after. His character at once enclosed by obsession and then again regal in complication, his being scarred like his face when Ishmael at last sees him, scarred from a wound or a birthmark, nature's inexpungible marking. His ivory leg fashioned from a whalebone announces his presence as he hobbles on the deck or stands in a hole in the wood to give his monologues, his commands, his orations; his language not practical or plain, but outsized, gorgeous in adjective and noun as he asserts or muses, when alone, the images of his "close-coiled woe."

As a Captain, Ahab is moody, but he is not a debased, bureaucratic tyrant, a flogger, a drunkard. Ahab's tyranny is that of a mob leader who persuades others to follow by the force of his own excitability, fearless of consequence; he is sometimes fearful to behold and lashes out as in a scene with Stubbs, the cheerful second mate. "Down, dog, and kennel!" he says in a fit of temper. And we note that Stubbs answers, "I am not used to be spoken to that way, sir; I do but less than half like it, sir." To which Ahab answers, "Avast!" without further rebuke.

In spite of a certain "sultanism of his brain," the captain of the *Pequod* was "the least given to that sort of shallowest assumption, and though the only homage he ever exacted was implicit, instantaneous obedience; though he required no man to remove his shoes ere stepping upon the quarter-deck; and though there were times when, owing to peculiar circumstances connected with events hereafter to be detailed, he addressed them in unusual terms, whether of condescension or *in terrorem* or otherwise; yet even Captain Ahab was by no means unobservant of the paramount forms and usages of the sea."

And yet Ishmael, observing the mercurial master of the destiny of those trapped in the "domestic peculiarity on shipboard," cannot withstand the waves of emotion the portentous creature evokes:

But, Ahab, my Captain, still moves before me in all his Nantucket grimness and shagginess; and in this episode touching Emperors and Kings, I must not conceal that I have only to do with a poor old whale-hunter like him; and, therefore, all outward majestical trappings and housings are denied me. Oh, Ahab! what shall be grand in thee, it must be plucked at from the skies, and dived for in the deep, and featured in the unbodied air!

Before the actual sighting of Moby Dick and the three-day chase ending in the whale's triumphant stoving of the *Pequod* and the death foreseen by Starbuck for himself, for Ahab, for all except Ishmael, there is an azure, steel-blue streak of pity and loss, of remembrance. All so late as to be mournful and unforgiving in the lyricism of the moment before the dirge.

Slowly crossing the deck from the scuttle, Ahab leaned over the side and watched how his shadow in the water sank and sank to his gaze, the more and more that he strove to pierce the profundity; but the lovely aromas in the enchanted air did at least seem to dispel, for a moment, the cantankerous thing in his soul. That glad, happy air, that winsome sky, did at last stroke and caress him; the step-mother world, so long and cruel–forbidding–now threw affectionate arms round his stubborn neck, and did seem to joyously sob over him, as if over one, that however willful and erring, she could yet find it in her heart to save and to bless. From beneath his slouched hat Ahab dropped a tear into the sea; nor did all the Pacific contain such wealth as that one wee drop.

And Ahab: his forty years come back to him; out of the forty, only three spent ashore. The formal isolation of a captain: "guinea-coast slavery of solitary command."

Away, whole oceans away, from that young girl I wedded past fifty, and sailed for Cape Hope the next day, leaving but one dent in my marriage pillow—wife? wife?—rather a widow with her husband alive. Aye, I widowed that poor girl when I married her, Starbuck; and then, the madness, the frenzy the boiling blood and the smoking brow, with which for a thousand lowerings old Ahab has furiously, foamingly chased his prey—more a demon than a man!—aye, aye! what a forty years, fool—old fool, has old Ahab been.

He asks Starbuck to come near him so that he may look into a "human eye," and tells him to stay on board when "branded Ahab gives the chase to Moby Dick." Starbuck remembers his own children and urges Ahab to turn back. But in vain: The inscrutable thing commands "that against all natural lovings and longings, I so keep pushing, and crowding, and jamming myself on all the time."

The singularity of Ahab, his stonelike substance with its elaborate Gothic ornamentation, has an accent of antiquity, as if he were a king in an old tragedy. In the enclosed world of nineteenth-century seagoing, Ahab is a king, living for forty years in the solitude of "the masoned walled-town of a Captain's exclusiveness, which admits but small entrance to any sympathy from the ocean country without." He is the king of the unstable principality, the *Pequod,* with its attendants, servitors, drinking water for a year, foodstuffs, buckets, a carpenter, a blacksmith and his forge to fix Ahab's splintered whalebone leg. The whalebone leg, emblem of an incapacity not to be borne but a violently degrading necessity, comes from a mighty captured whale and, as if in a special malice, is far from stable. "This is hard which should be soft, and that is soft which should be hard." So Ahab cries out in his crippled fury.

The White Whale has taken the leg as a trophy and also in a faraway extension of power taken the old Captain's manhood!

> For it had not been long prior to the *Pequod*'s sailing from Nantucket, that he had been found one night lying prone upon the ground, and insensibly; by some unknown, and seemingly inexplicable, unimaginable casualty, his ivory limb having been so violently displaced, that it had stake-wise smitten, and all but pierced his groin; nor was it without extreme difficulty that the agonizing wound was entirely cured.

Ishmael, the young man from Manhattan, is the moral center of the book, a work tantalizingly subversive and yet somehow if not affirming at least forgiving of the blind destructiveness of human nature and of nature itself. Before leaving for the sea, Ishmael had been full of spleen and "pausing before coffin warehouses," that is, thinking of suicide. Going to sea is a revival of the will to live and to experience what may come.

As the "I," the first-person narrator, Ishmael drifts in and out and certainly does not practice a strict "point of view," which would indeed be a crippling of Melville's resolute discursiveness and inspiration in the lonely soliloquies and tirades of Ahab and in such scenes as Starbuck with the tempting musket. The contemplation of life and death, the vastness of the landscape, the mountainous detail, the rush and violence of the human explosion of energy, and the defiant surge of protective will by Moby Dick—all of that is Melville himself as narrator sitting for a twelve-hour stint of composition in the Berkshires.

Ishmael, civilized, a white American, a common seaman, not an officer and not a castaway, not an *isolato,* is rational and sometimes rationalizing; he is not immune to the force of Ahab's lurid dream of a kind of court justice in which his loss is that of a victim and the White Whale is the culprit to be, as it were, apprehended and sentenced to a retributive death. But then, in a chapter of great imaginative power, "*The Grand Armada,*" the whales appear in a herd, "reposing," displaying a "wondrous fearlessness and confidence, or else a still becharmed panic which it was impossible not to marvel at." They become creatures at home, clinging together, the females giving birth:

> But far beneath this wondrous world upon the surface, another and still stranger world met our eyes as we gazed over the side. For, suspended in those watery vaults, floated the forms of the nursing mothers of the whales, and those that by their enormous girth seemed shortly to become mothers. The lake, as I have hinted,

was to a considerable depth exceedingly transparent; and as human infants while suckling will calmly and fixedly gaze away from the breast, as if leading two different lives at the time; and while yet drawing mortal nourishment, be still spiritually feasting upon some unearthly reminiscence;—even so did the young of these whales seem looking up towards us, but not at us, as if we were but a bit of Gulf-weed in their new-born sight. . . . The delicate side-fins, and the palms of his flukes, still freshly retained the plaited crumpled appearance of a baby's ears newly arrived from foreign parts.

The sea, its awful, challenging infinitude, and the soothing, hypnotic balm of a clear day and gentle waves—you sometimes feel as you read *Moby-Dick* that these dichotomies of the ocean almost drove Melville mad. In his book he must put everything: "The masterless ocean overruns the globe." He notes that the sea has not been friendly to man: It will "insult and murder him and pulverize the stateliest, stiffest frigate he can make." And then the sea is not a "friend to its own offspring." And yet again, in the same paragraphs, "consider the almost devilish brilliance and beauty of many of its most remorseless tribes, as the dainty embellished shape of the many species of shark."

And on a transparent blue day, one of the harpooners thought he had seen the White Whale himself. No, not the whale; what was seen was the giant squid, "the most wondrous phenomenon which the secret seas have hitherto revealed to man."

A vast pulpy mass, furlongs in the length and breadth, of a glancing cream-color, lay floating on the water, innumerable long arms radiating from its center, and curling and twisting like a nest of anacondas, as if blindly to clutch at any hapless object within reach. No perceptible face or front did it have; no conceivable token of either sensation or instinct; but undulated there on the billows, an unearthly, formless, chance-like apparition of life.

The ambiguity, the inconstancy, the incongruity of the natural world and the wish to give a microscopic account of the creature that shares equality on the stage with Ahab: that is, the sperm whale.

The view of the full front of its head is "sublime."

But in the great Sperm Whale, this high and mighty god-like dignity inherent in the brow is so immensely amplified that gazing upon it, in that full front view, you feel the Deity and the dread powers more forcibly than in beholding any other object in living nature. . . . Physiognomy, like every other human science, is but a passing fable. If, then, Sir William Jones, who read in thirty languages, could not read the simplest peasant's face in its profounder and more subtle meanings, how may unlettered Ishmael hope to read the awful Chaldee of the Sperm Whale's brow? I but put that brow before you. Read it if you can.

Sublimity, godlike deity, the White Whale, rare, its milky foam, the gathering upon its hulk of mountainous superstitions: immortality, ubiquity, "encountered in opposite latitudes at one and the same instant of time. . . ." Ahab, his leg reaped away by Moby Dick, "as a mower a blade of grass," had come to identify with the White Whale "not only all his bodily woes, but all his intellectual and spiritual exasperations." Crazy Ahab, Ishmael believes, had piled upon the White Whale's hump the sum of all the general rage and hate felt by his whole race from Adam down.

Probing into the mystery of Ahab, Melville fashions a complex progression of his hurts into monomania, a subtle, even sly, growth within Ahab himself. As he lay, after the wounding, in his hammock on the ship bound for home, his ravings became so terrifying, the mates placed him in a straitjacket; at last the delirium seemed to subside in his outward actions, appeared to tell of healing. But this was the remaining surface of sanity, the consciousness of the world about that told him to dissemble the inscrutable violence within him, and thus he was given a new command and sent out on the *Pequod*.

The Whiteness of the Whale: "It was the whiteness of the whale that above all things appalled me." So speaks Ishmael in this incomparable chapter that calls upon Melville's reading but most of all on his creative strength in constructing a sort of anxious foundation for what he has offered in this strange fable. So evanescent and paradoxical is whiteness that one does feel a struggle in Melville's contemplation, not a struggle of incapacity but for aesthetic definition, for containment. The White Whale: As D. H. Lawrence wrote: "Of course he is a symbol. Of what? I doubt even Melville knew exactly. That's the best of it."

Loveliness of whiteness in natural objects: marbles, japonicas, and pearls; royalty mounted on their white elephants or chargers; the innocence of brides; the white ermine of judges; sacramental vestments.

Yet consider the white bear of the poles and the white shark of the tropics, the whiteness of the albatross. "The disguise of whiteness makes bloody creatures more horrible. The marble pallor of the dead, ghosts rising in the milk-white fog." By way of an idiosyncratic stretch, "to the man of untutored ideality, . . . the bare mention of Whitsuntide marshal in the fancy such long, dreary, speechless processions of slow-pacing pilgrims, down-cast and hooded with new-fallen snow." For the Protestant of Middle America, the passing of a White Friar or a White Nun "evoke such an eyeless statue in the soul." The White Mountains of New Hampshire, with their splendid heights, in certain moods, arouse a "gigantic ghastliness over the soul." The Antarctic sailor, cold and endangered, sees the waters around him as a "boundless church-yard grinning upon him with its lean ice monuments and splintered crosses."

On and on Melville goes, aware of the insubstantiality of this search for whiteness; a "dumb blankness"; the "colorless, all-color of atheism from which we shrink"; the "palsied universe lies before us as a leper. . . . And of all these things the Albino whale was the symbol. Wonder ye then at the fiery hunt."

The White Whale, ambiguously innocent as a virgin bride, ambiguously rapacious as the white shark of the tropics, is here a fictional creation of unparalleled inspiration.

So grand is Melville's struggle to give verbal life to his vision that the reader partakes of the consummation with some trembling of the aesthetic senses, as if he, too, might be overwhelmed by the beautiful difficulty of the apprehending and conceptualizing.

And so it is with the split psyche of Ahab, pitiful, old, scorched-browed demon, himself bewitched. "Gifted with the high perception, I lack the low, enjoying power." Ahab's language, a grandiose, extravagant word intoxication in a fierce battle with the shape of his lacerated feelings. His language is the signal of the *Pequod*'s anarchy in which Ahab is both the aroused victim of a remaining tyrant and the executioner ready with the blade, the commanding Robespierre.

Is Ahab, Ahab? Is it I, God, or who that lifts this arm? But if the great sun move not of himself, but is an errand boy in heaven; nor one single star can revolve, but by some invisible power; how then can this one small heart beat; this one small brain think thoughts; unless God does that beating, does that thinking, does that living and not I . . . Who's to doom, when the judge himself is dragged to the bar?

The cadence, the compositional rhythms and elevated tone, cause many to think of *Moby-Dick* as an epic poem even though Ahab with the business of the crew is just a shouting whaler: "Lower away then d'ye hear? Spread yourselves, give way, all four boats, pull more to leeward"–and so on. Melville was, no matter, writing a novel, one with no antecedents at hand. The informational chapters, cetology, are *written,* sometimes in mock bibliographical fashion: Folio, Octavo, Duodecimo; amusing Melvillian descriptive touches: "The white comprises part of his head, and the whole of his mouth which makes him look as if he had just escaped from a felonious visit to a meal-bag": this, the mealy-mouthed porpoise. Few readers have any knowledge of a whale beyond a visit to a papier-mâché carcass hanging on a museum wall, and the inserted information is not an excrescence but takes its place in the fiction very much like the family history, grandparents, forebears of the central characters in conventional fiction. In this imaginative, developing story the whale is a central character, a human antagonist, as it were.

Short chapters, a rush of new plot turns, reversals, not flung into the frame as filler or detritus but to reappear down the line with the assurance of fictional craft. Queequeg is taken ill, very ill, and felt to be so near death that the method of his disposal, his watery funeral, is at hand. Poor Queequeg remembered having seen in Nantucket that little canoes were provided for the dead to be "floated away to the starry archipelagoes." On the *Pequod* the dead were tossed in their hammocks to the "death-devouring shark," as was the custom at the time. Appropriate wood was found, and the carpenter, taking Queequeg's exact measurement, executed the dying wish. Interment honored, Queequeg suddenly revived and "with his wildwhimsiness"

used the coffin for a sea chest and spent his spare hours
carving on it obscure figures and drawings very much
like the tattoos on his body. This diversion will, at the
end of the book, find its meaning in a magical resolution.
With the lowerings for the chase, the lifeboat is lost in the
sea; and when boat and all in it are drowned, the lone survivor, Ishmael, is saved by using the chest as a lifeboat
and drifting to safety, cradled by the dead Queequeg, if
you like.

Whaling ships meeting in the waters of the cruising
grounds sometimes had the custom of social exchanges
between the officers, although Captain Ahab, locked in his
inward dialogue, had no heart for such courtesy unless
there be news of Moby Dick. There is a meeting with a
Nantucket whaler named *Jeroboam,* under Captain Mayhew. The captain will not come aboard the *Pequod* for
fear of bringing down on it the epidemic on his own ship;
but Ahab has no fear of the epidemic because the *Jeroboam* has sighted Moby Dick. The real plague on the unlucky ship is the presence of a mad crewman who thinks
he is the angel Gabriel and who has created the same
vertiginous disorder as Ahab himself on the *Pequod.* With
his assumption of divinity and the opening of his magic
vials, one containing laudanum, Gabriel has brought the
crew to his side and to a threat of mutiny if Captain
Mayhew should try to unload the madman at the next
port.

With the sighting of Moby Dick, Macey, the chief
mate, "burned with ardor to encounter him" despite
Gabriel's prophecy of doom should he do so. The mate

poised his lance, but the whale was triumphant, and "the mate forever sank." As for Ahab's determination to hunt the White Whale, Gabriel vehemently predicted his doom: "Think, think of the blasphemer–dead, and down there!–beware of the blasphemer's end!"

Meeting the *Virgin,* or the *Jungfrau:* a German ship, a comically inefficient vessel, hunting the whale but needing to borrow oil for the ship's lamps. The captain of the *Virgin* does not know the difference between a sperm whale and a finback, "uncapturable because of its incredible power of swimming."

The *Rosebud:* a French whaler and therefore in search of ambergris for the scents beloved of the nation. However, the *Rosebud* emits foul odors as she approaches, the trouble being that it has a whale alongside that died a natural death and is of no value except to befoul the air of the vessel in search of the fragrant ambergris.

The *Samuel Enderby* of London: In this encounter, the national American pride that has seen the German and French whalers in theatrical, comical ignorance of the profession subsides when the answer to Captain Ahab's refrain, "Hast seen the White Whale?" brings a more interesting reply. The captain has seen the whale and lost an arm to it. His response is to avoid it, but Ahab in a frenzy cries out, "Man the boat! Which way heading?"

The *Bachelor:* a Nantucket ship heading home in great jubilation; so much whale oil in the hold, hardly room for anything else. "Hast seen the White Whale?" The answer: "No; only heard of him; but don't believe in him at all." Ahab cried out, "Set all sail!" His thought on the *Bachelor* as his crew looks with grave, lingering glances toward the celebrating, receding vessel: "Thou art a full ship and homeward bound, thou sayest; well, then, call me an empty ship, and outward-bound. So go thy ways, and I will mine."

A weary pathos in Ahab's unrelenting grip on his destiny profoundly complicates Melville's creation of this hero of a tragedy with no more models than the waves of the sea. Ahab has no home; Nantucket, the young wife and child on the widow's walk looking toward the sea for his return, cannot arouse in him an active nostalgia, a fireside humanity. A dying ship on the sea is his domicile, his dwelling place, and to this Starbuck's grieving longing for his wife, his daughter, is a threat.

The *Rachel:* This interlude in which Ahab confronts the deepest human misery of family loss, parental suffering, and love for another leaves him unmoved. Although he has a child, he is not a father, has no existential grasp of the sacred tie. "Hast seen the White Whale?" Once more the musical, thematic signature. The answer: "Aye, yesterday. Have ye seen a whale-boat adrift?" The captain of the strange boat was a Nantucketer he knew. But still, ever, Captain Ahab has no greeting, no recognition in his heart except for the whale. The whale, was it killed, and no, not killed.

The *Rachel*'s story is told; a sighting of Moby Dick, the boats in pursuit; the whale escaped, three boats at last recovered, one missing throughout the night. The captain's object in boarding the *Pequod* was to ask help in finding the missing boat. It developed that the captain's twelve-year-old son was on the missing boat. "My boy, my own boy is among them." Beseeching, he reminds the icy Ahab that he too has a boy, "a child of his old age."

Ahab orders his boat to continue its course. "Even now I lose time. Good bye, good bye. God bless ye, man, and may I forgive myself, but I must go."

At last the three-day chase for Moby Dick begins. He is there, "the glistening white shadow from his broad, milky forehead"; "the blue waters interchangeably flowed over into the moving valley of his steady wake; and on either hand bright bubbles arose and danced by his side." The chase, its end foreordained, its moments of a glittering horror as each man, the cast, dies his own death one by one, with Stubbs thinking of "one red cherry" and hoping his mother has drawn his pay; Starbuck, the final, grasping assertion of a reasonable victim as if pleading with a murderer: a murderer with a knife at his victim's throat:

"Oh! Ahab, not too late is it, even now, the third day, to desist. See! Moby Dick seeks thee not. It is thou, thou, that madly seekest him!" And Ahab, on the final day, choked to death as the rope grabs him about the neck and the dreadful scream: "The ship? Great God, where is the ship?" "All its crew, and each floating oar, and every lance-pole; and spinning, animate and inanimate, all round and round in one vortex, carried the smallest chip of the *Pequod* out of sight." And the great shroud of the sea rolled on as it rolled five thousand years ago.

A coda of ravishing beauty, Ishmael's word. In the roiling waters, he somehow found that Queequeg's coffin, now used to replace the lost life buoy, "floated by my side."

Buoyed up by that coffin, for almost one whole day and
night, I floated on a soft and dirge-like main. The un-
harming sharks, they glided by as if with padlocks on
their mouths; the savage sea-hawks sailed with sheathed
beaks. On the second day, a sail drew near, nearer, and
picked me up at last. It was the devious-cruising *Rachel,*
that in her retracing search after her missing children,
only found another orphan.

And so it was, completed, dedicated, a noble dramatic
tragedy, if not for the stage. Moby Dick is an antagonist
without knowledge of the plot; a great creature, innocent,
blind, unaware of its name, its role, its past transgression,
and finally, in the field of battle, perhaps a mistaken White
Whale, knowing only the indifferent harpoons flashing
out from the hostile, death-eager boats. In his way, Melville does, against reason, make Moby Dick a character,
rival of Ahab's for dignity, power, and even honor. The
House of Moby Dick and the House of Ahab, ancient
feuds. The cast, on board, like sea chests with secret be-
longings: Pip, a boy damaged by the sea and intermit-
tently cradled by Ahab; Fedellah, an Asiatic demonic
intrusion, a companion urging Ahab to destruction for the
black glory of it.

And Ahab himself, a weary sailor too long alone and
homeless, created by the strange industry of whaling that
is soon to be outmoded and its rigors forgotten. In the
end, Ahab justifies the instruction, the history of the enterprise, the lessons in cetology because, interesting in

themselves, they have changed a New England seaman into a monomaniac without land memories.

Moby-Dick received favorable notices in the English and American press, noting the "humor," the descriptive elegance, originality of conception; others predictably fretted about the "irreverence," the formlessness. Most distressing to the author was a notice by his friend, Duyckinck, in the important *Literary World;* a document of inattention, casual praise with stronger condemnation for the faults of exaggerated mannerisms, "piratical running down of creeds and opinions, the conceited indifferentism of Emerson, or the run-a-muck style of Carlyle."

Family, *Pierre,* "Benito Cereno,"
"Bartleby, the Scrivener"

WHEN THE BOOK BECAME, almost a century later, the object of the best critics of American literature, the language, the interpretation, the exegesis, fell upon it like moonbeams in a bright sky: Faustian, Promethean, archetypal, Shakespearean, biblical, Homeric.

Melville's second son, Stanwix, was born a few weeks after the publication of *Moby-Dick.* He is a puzzle and will not be a gratifying son, heir to the family of great names, if not much in worldly goods. Stanwix, two years younger than Malcolm, was in the house years later when Malcolm, at eighteen, died of a gunshot wound to his head. Stanwix left home, went here and there on boats, a wanderer, a drifter. Deafness fell upon him at the time of Malcolm's death, a strange suddenness of onset and a handicap in the employment world. He ended up in California, estranged, ill of tuberculosis, which killed him at the age of thirty-five. The biographer Ms. Robertson-Lorant notes that he died with a male friend at his side. That is of no consequence unless it means to suggest a homosexual companionship.

Malcolm's young habits had been the cause of concern in a routine way. On the night before his death, he did not come home until 3 A.M. His mother was waiting up for him. He went to bed, locked his door, and did not arise the next morning, but answered the knock. Later, there was no answer, but nothing was done until Melville came home late in the evening, broke down the door, and found his son dead from a self-inflicted wound. Lizzie Melville insisted he had shown no signs of drunkenness the night before; indeed, both parents maintained that he was not at any time likely to drink, that he was an unusually sober young man at all times. They mourned him as a lost paragon. He died in 1867 when his father's career as a prose writer had been abandoned for poems and for his daily service for hire as a customs inspector.

The Melvilles had two daughters; the older, Bessie, suffered from severe rheumatoid arthritis and remained at home, unmarried, to be cared for by her mother. Frances, the last child, had a more traditional and certainly more consoling passage through life. She married young, and married well enough, had daughters and granddaughters who would become solicitous about Melville's papers and legacy. The cabin boy became a family man, or at least a man with a family, one always at home, but hardly the man of the house, with his scullery routine of writing at frightening speed, as if driven by a tyrannical overseer.

"Dollars damn me," he said. Insulting advances from the publisher, dwindling sales, feckless reviewers—and did he still hope for dollars in the dismaying progression from *Moby-Dick,* publication on October 18, 1851, to *Pierre,* publication on August 6, 1852? A Grub Street journeyman; that didn't please, try this? *Pierre,* the bottom of the bag, perhaps a satire on the ladies' popular fiction of the day; but it is ill designed as a tease, a throwaway, being as it is very long, heavily plotted, ornately declamatory, wildly unreal. The windswept *Wuthering Heights* had been published in 1847, five years previous to *Pierre,* and it could be wished, if Melville were drawn to exorcising demons, that he had read Emily Brontë; he had not.

Many critics will find much of interest in *Pierre:* the slaying of the consuming mother, idol smashing of the once-revered dead father, the looming threat of conventional marriage, the mysterious thread of an illegitimate sister, murder of the presumed bride's brother, and in the end all the bodies piled up on the stage. Pierre: "Lo, I leave corpses wherever I go."

Specialists, particularly those in the academic institutions, take a proprietary and protective attitude toward those authors in, as it were, their care. Thematic structures, always beguiling in the shadowy Melville, may loom over the execution; however, the mysterious follies in *Pierre* were seized by his contemporary critics as a personal affront to be expressed in adjectives of murderous intent. "Leering demonical aspect"; "trash of conception, execution, dialogue and sentiment"; "muddy, foul, and corrupt"; "Herman Melville Crazy"; "gone 'clean daft.' "

Pierre, at the opening, is living in the country with his mother, Mary Glendinning. He is strangely enough a Gansevoort, since his grandfather is said to have held a fort against the "murderous half-breed Brandt." Nothing further is made of this, and it is perhaps a joke inserted only for the family amusement. In any case, as a Glendinning, Pierre is a true aristocrat of American lineage grander than the English peerage, "manufactured by George III in the hundreds." He is in his teens, and his mother, at fifty, is still beautiful, widowed, flirtatious, and managing. The son and the mother address each other as brother and sister:

"Don't be so ridiculous, brother Pierre; so you are going to take Lucy that long ride among the hills this morning? She is a sweet girl, a most lovely girl."

"Yes, that is rather my opinion, sister Mary—By heavens, mother, the five zones hold not such another!"

Lucy and Pierre are engaged; she is of a fortune called "ample" and has the further dynastic advantage of being the daughter of the best friend of Pierre's father, both the fathers being conveniently deceased. Gothic elements descend on the fiction like a hailstorm, scattering pellets of confusion, mystery, accusation, complications from the grave reappearing to assault the living. Haunting faces disturb the dallying, summering Pierre. One, the face of a young girl seen sewing at the modest house of village ladies, will alarm Pierre for reasons "he knows not why"; at home the double portraits of his father, the regimental, and a small, somewhat more abandoned visage disliked by the mother will disturb him. Soon he will receive a letter from the sewing girl, signed: "Thy sister, Isabel."

The novel, with flamboyant scenes in New York, will proceed to the disaster foreordained for all in the plot and to the disaster for Melville. A hysterical burlesque as the pages make their weary way; improbable rantings, love scenes of a shape that suggest words to an inert mannequin lolling in a window:

> Thou are made of that fine, unshared stuff of which God makes his seraphim. By thy divine devotedness to me, is met by mine to thee. . . . Harken, harken to me. I seek not now to gain thy prior assent to a thing as yet undone; but I will call to thee now, Isabel, from the depth of a foregone act to ratify it backward by thy consent.

The most interesting aspect of *Pierre* will be: Why was it written? What did Melville wish for it? The overwhelming sadness of the enterprise is on behalf of the author, the honorable, gifted, madly driven man, forever at his desk. He was punished gleefully in the manner of literary assassinations.

Raging disappointment, self-doubt hard to escape when it is the intention of the insults in the press, exhaustion, the distracting and silently accusing household, such as it must be to a battered, unlikely father; insolvency of long acquaintance but rapping on the door as if to a merely absentminded debtor who must accept an overlooked bill—in these years Melville is still of a creative energy uncanny in its perseverance.

Between the publication of *Pierre* and yet another novel, *Israel Potter,* he will answer a request to write shorter pieces, not very short they are, for the magazine *Putnam's,* a publication that paid well and perhaps for that reason went ultimately into bankruptcy. He produced "Bartleby, the Scrivener" in 1853; "The Encantadas" in 1854; "Benito Cereno" in 1855, to be gathered in *Piazza Tales* in 1856. The family, we understand, was worried about his condition. It is very hard to live with one so desperately stretched, pummeled, weary, frazzled and fractious, but more dreadful to live *in* such a state than to live *with* it. This old man of letters was thirty-six years old.

The Encantadas, the Galápagos Islands, off Ecuador in the Pacific: Here the descriptive language makes its desolate claim with a fierce power. The volcanic island looks as the world might "after a penal conflagration"; "like split Syrian gourds left withering in the sun"; of the giant land tortoises, "there is something strangely self-condemned in the appearance of these creatures. Lasting sorrow and penal hopelessness are in no animal form so suppliantly expressed as in theirs." There are "prostrate trunks of blasted pines"; "bandit birds with long bills cruel as daggers."

"Benito Cereno," an adaptation of a narrative published in 1817 by Captain Amasa Delano of Duxbury, Massachusetts, is a dramatic, suspenseful tale of the belligerent forces in human nature, and in history. Captain Delano is the blinkered, resolutely lifelike star of the narration. He is cheerful, friendly, and above all, a thoroughly American fellow cast for a time adrift by the inchoate and alien, by a beleaguered, paralyzed Spanish captain, and by mysterious blacks from Africa. While anchored off the coast of Chile, he sees a woeful, floundering vessel "carrying Negro slaves from one port to another," for sale, as cargo. On the decks of the disreputably unkempt ship, a jumble of blacks and whites in hapless disarray; the captain, Don Benito, a young Spaniard, standing by in a "spiritless manner among the din and chaos." The good Delano from his own well-kept larder brings provisions and water and boards the distressed ship to inquire; his own boat for a time is caught in a wind, and so he must wait for its return. During the wait the drama unfolds.

There is a young black man who appears to be acting as a valet to Don Benito, carefully holding him up as he seems near to fainting and in a bewildering scene giving him his daily shave, which to Delano is a superfluous nicety. Don Benito shows a lack of expressive gratitude for the effort Delano has made on his behalf; his "reserve" is thought a rudeness and his lack of control of the ship an insult to marine protocol. There are apparitions about, mainly a huge African with an iron collar about his neck. But throughout it is the elegant and insinuating attentiveness of Babo, the "valet," that arouses Captain Delano's imagination and approbation. With a smile and in jest he says, "I would like to have your man myself—what will you take for him? Would fifty doubloons be any object?" Babo, bowing, replies that he would not part from "master" for a thousand doubloons.

In certain exchanges, Benito will, in his "Iberian" languor, say that he owes his life to Babo, and the attendant will gracefully demur: Babo is nothing, what Babo has done is only his duty—and so on. Captain Delano is altogether elated by the faithful fellow. "Don Benito, I envy you such a friend; slave I cannot call him." In his musings he will decide what such faithful acts have gained for the Negro race: "the repute of making the most pleasing body servant in the world; one, too, with whom a master need not be on stiffly superior terms, but may treat with familiar trust; less a body servant than a devoted companion."

What Melville has created in the vividly convincing Captain Delano is a vigorous, kindly gentleman of the end of the eighteenth century who will approach the black race in a mood of complacent, condescending human fellowship. "In fact Captain Delano took to Negroes, not philanthropically but genially, like other men to Newfoundland dogs." What he feels and manifests is not so much sinful as debilitating to his judgment of what is actually at hand.

It will turn out that the ship is the scene of a slave revolt. Captain Benito is a hostage with a knife at his throat, and the obsequious Babo is the leader of the rebels, determined to return the ship to Senegal, that is, to freedom. Delano's men, with their guns and the remaining Spanish sailors, take the ship, killing some Negroes even though "to kill or maim the Negroes was not the object"; they are still valuable as slave commerce. Melville then shifts his narration to the existing court records of the rebellion and to the depositions taken in Lima. Don Benito does not recover and still wastes away:

> "You are saved," cried Captain Delano, more and more astonished and pained, "you are saved; what cast such a shadow upon you?"
> "The Negro."

A mournful tale of misapprehension, kindly in the beginning, leading to retributive "justice," which is death for

Babo, death for some of the conspirators, reenslavement for the remainder. Melville has taken a historical incident and with a cool, remote imagination uncovered the secrets of racism. Babo's extraordinary sinuosity, sadistic as it is, his theatricalism, the "hive of subtlety" that is his rampant intelligence and imagination, have in this telling of the plot altered the African image of the period. Babo is hanged, his body turned, except for his head, to ashes. The final line, the last words: "The head, that hive of subtlety, fixed on a pole, met, unabashed, the gaze of the whites."

"Bartleby, the Scrivener":* a work of austere minimalism, of philosophical quietism, of radical literary shape, of consummate despair, and withal beautiful in the perfection of the telling. "A Story of Wall Street" is the subtitle; the scene, a "snug" law firm doing business "among rich men's bonds and mortgages and title deeds." The narrator, a mild man of the law, elderly and soon to retire, begins to think about the law copyists, or scriveners, he has known in his thirty years of practice. He is a gentleman, modest, recognizing his own little vanities, one of which is that he has done business with John Jacob Astor and likes to mention his name, "for it hath a rounded and orbicular sound to it and rings like unto bullion." In his dealings with Bartleby, he will be touched for the first time in his life by "overpowering, stinging melancholy . . . a fraternal melancholy."

*A revision of my essay previously published in *Bartleby in Manhattan,* 1983.

A copying demand had led the lawyer to run an advertisement in search of an employee, and this brought to him Bartleby, a young man, sedate, "pallidly neat, pitiably respectable." Bartleby's desk faces a brick wall, without a view, a suitable place for one who has no "views" of the outside world. He begins copying as if "long famishing for something to copy," although the lawyer observes that he does it "silently, palely, mechanically." On the third day of copying, he is asked to collaborate in the matter of proofreading. The laconic, implacable signature is at hand, the mysterious utterance that cannot be interpreted and cannot be misunderstood. Bartleby replies, "I would prefer not to."

The lawyer's disbelief provides the occasion for "I would prefer not to" soon to be repeated three times and "with no uneasiness, anger, impatience or impertinence." By the singularity of response, the absence of "because," this negative domination seizes the story like a sudden ambush in the streets.

Bartleby would prefer not to read proof with his employer; a little later he would prefer not to examine his own quadruplicate copyings with the help of other clerks; he would prefer not to consider that this communal proofreading is laborsaving and customary. About his "mulish vagary"—no answer.

In Bartleby's replies there is no coquetry; it is merely candid, final, inflexible. Above all it is not "personal"; not an objection to the collaborators and not to the activity of proofreading itself. The lawyer will struggle throughout the tale to fill up the hole, to search for "personality." Bartleby is always alone, in an utter loneliness that pierces the lawyer's heart when it turns out that Bartleby has no home at all but is living in the office at night. He is in no way a citizen of Manhattan or a consumer of its wares; he shuns the streets and eats only ginger nuts. He is starving himself to death.

Bartleby, in his mute way, is a master of language. The lawyer, trying to pierce the shroud of communication, will wish to change the copyist's style. Instead of *prefer* not, he proposes *will* not but the corrective answer returns; I *prefer not*. What is the difference between *will not* and *prefer not?* Bartleby has chosen, and his language is what he is. And then, standing at "the dead-wall window," he announces that he will do no more copying. No more. The lawyer notices the appearance of eyestrain, but Melville does not wish the progression to enter the region of causality. And it does not do so. Bartleby is asked to be a little reasonable, and the response: "At present I would prefer not to be a little reasonable"—a "mildly cadaverous reply."

The baffled lawyer considers dismissing Bartleby, but he cannot, not even after "no more copying." He thinks: "I should have as soon thought of turning my pale, plaster-of-paris bust of Cicero out of doors." As a "merely social visitor to Trinity Church," he ponders the idea that he is somehow predestined to have Bartleby, but decides not, and it is at last clear that Bartleby must go with a generous bonus, every sort of accommodation, and good wishes. The lawyer returns the next morning, and Bartleby is still there, the offered money not picked up.

"Will you not quit me?"

"I would prefer *not* to quit you."

In desperation, the office is packed up for a move. New tenants arrived and found Bartleby sitting on the banister. They turn him out, or seek to, but he remains "sitting on the banister." Bartleby's reduced language has turned the poor lawyer to extreme metaphors and to think of him as "the last column of some ruined temple" and "a bit of wreck in the mid-Atlantic." He begins to imagine new occupations; a clerkship in a dry-goods store, but Bartleby declines, adding, "But I am not particular." A bartender, a bill collector, a companion to a young man traveling abroad—ludicrous imaginings, as the lawyer knows.

No, Bartleby will not, "but I am not particular." By the phrase, Bartleby seems to wish to keep the lawyer from the tedium of error. Bartleby himself is particular in that he is a thing distinguished from another, but he is not particular in being fastidious, choosy. He is at last arrested and sent to the Tombs.

A prison visit is made, and the kindly lawyer, in his therapeutic hope, tells the scrivener not to despair; the charge is not a disgrace, and even in prison one may sometimes see the sky and a patch of green. Bartleby replies: "I know where I am." He refuses food—"I am unused to dinners"—and thus he dies. Not quite the end for the lawyer, with his compassion, his need to unearth some scrap of buried personality or private history. We have the beautiful coda Melville has written, a laying to rest of Bartleby and of the graceful curiosity and insatiable charity of the Wall Street lawyer. A rumor:

The report was this: that Bartleby had been a subordinate clerk in the Dead Letter Office at Washington, from which he had been suddenly removed by a change in administration. . . . Dead letters! does it not sound like dead men? Conceive a man by nature and misfortune prone to a pallid hopelessness, can any business seem more fitted to heighten it than that of continually handling these dead letters, and assorting them for the flames? . . . On errands of life, these letters speed to death. . . . Ah, Bartleby! Ah, humanity!

Withdrawal, dead letters; fortunately for this Antarctic expedition no sources have been found under the scholar's hoe. The "fraternal melancholy" lay at hand. Along with *Moby-Dick* and *Billy Budd,* "Bartleby, the Scrivener" forms, a century and a half later, the trio of Melville's most revered work.

Marriage, *The Confidence-Man*

AFTER THE FLOGGING of *Pierre* in 1852, the birth of a third child, the daughter Bessie, the irritable householder of the forlorn copyrights was, as we can read in biographies, drinking when he felt like it and an obstructive, unaccommodating mate for the daughter of a wildly accommodating Judge Shaw. Elizabeth Shaw had married a man of very singular shape and occupation.

The historian Froude, writing a biography of Thomas Carlyle, could decide that *Carlyle ought not to have married.* This is a disorienting proclamation about one of the most famous and interesting unions of the Victorian age. Lizzie Melville is a sort of country wife by comparison with the childless Jane Carlyle, who was surrounded by friends, such as the Italian revolutionary Mazzini, and busy writing her witty and snooty letters about the dumbbell serving girls and the bedbugs. Melville's wife is burdened by the inescapable, unending chores of domestic life, one of which was the spectral Herman, whose books went forth, like his father's deals, only to be returned as just so much overstock. His appalling "celestial" labor and her earthbound servitude reduced them both to strange, well-born peons somehow landing in the cane fields. She is on occasion said to be "prostrate" and near collapse; among other tribulations she had to wait until fifteen years later for the death of his lashing overseer-mother, Maria Gansevoort Melville. But they carried on, although she will consult lawyers and her pastor about a divorce ten years later.

Meanwhile, henceforth, however it is to be phrased, there are two novels, *Israel Potter* and *The Confidence-Man*, and yet another daughter, Frances. The child, as an item of productivity, is more readily accounted for than the relentless procreative machine that clanked on and on in defiance of the marketplace. *Israel Potter* is an agreeable and readable book, not much read. The American Revolution, sacred to the genealogy of the Gansevoort and Melville clans, is the setting for "youthful adventures" of the devoted patriot Israel Potter, who left a pamphlet record for Melville to draw upon. The young Israel, forbidden by his father to marry his love, takes off like Peter Rabbit with his knapsack on a stick, hires out as a farmer, gets a gun and turns deer hunter, saves his money to buy a farm, sells out at a profit, goes to Canada as a peddler of skins and furs, sails on whaling voyages, his success as a harpooner and hunter preparing him for Bunker Hill. When Washington ordered recruits to man ships to interrupt British supplies coming over the water, Israel volunteers. The ship is captured, and Israel is sent to England, where he will escape to wander over London and Paris.

The most interesting things in the novel are the "portraits" of Benjamin Franklin, John Paul Jones, and Ethan Allen, each to be lampooned. D. H. Lawrence wrote about "snuff-colored" Franklin that "he made himself a list of

virtues, which he trotted inside like a gray nag in a pad-
dock." Israel, "after a curious adventure on the Pont
Neuf," meets Franklin, dressed like a music-hall sorcerer
and giving forth to poor Israel his ready homilies on the
matter of thrift. Franklin, "having weighed the world,
could act any part in it." And after warning Israel about a
pretty serving girl is himself "the caressed favorite of the
highest born beauties of the court."

John Paul Jones first appears in civilian dress, looking
like "a disinherited Indian Chief in European clothes."
There is a good deal of badinage between the naval hero
and Franklin before Jones takes the "good Yankee" Israel
Potter aboard for the great battle between the *Bon Homme
Richard* and the British frigate *Serapis*. Melville goes
through the battle in patriotic and marine detail before we
leave the victorious John Paul with "a light and dandified
air, switching his gold-headed cane, and throwing a passing arm around all the pretty chambermaids he encountered, kissing them resoundingly, as if saluting a frigate.
All barbarians are rakes."

Ethan Allen, the brawny Green Mountain boy, "Sam-
son among the Philistines," is another curious American
patriot, captured and shipped off to England. The hero of
Ticonderoga is such a braggart and Herculean outrage he
is shipped back to New York in an exchange of prisoners.

Israel Potter, wandering in exile for forty-five years,
"surpassed the forty years in the natural wilderness of the
outcast Hebrews under Moses." If Melville wrote this
book with his left hand, more or less, his combat with language is so victorious even here that his strength appears

his birthright like that of Ethan Allen, "a wild beast; but of a royal sort and unsubdued by the cage." London, which he calls the city of Dis:

> As in eclipses, the sun was hidden, the air darkened; the whole dull, dismayed aspect of things, as if some neighboring volcano, belching its premonitory smoke, were about to whelm the great town, as Herculaneum and Pompeii, or the Cities of the Plain. And as they had been upturned in terror towards the mountain, all faces were more or less snowed, or spotted with soot. Nor marble, nor flesh, nor the sad spirit of man, may in this cindery city of Dis abide white.

Ill health, overwork, the near certainty of failure; in the midst of the nagging hardship of living, art is a thing apart, or so it seems in the verve, the brio with which Melville in *The Confidence-Man* composed the crowded traffic jam of his boatload of native scoundrels, our own. An examination of the follies, the chicanery, the brazen dupery of mankind, lends itself to comic scenes with malicious intent; thus, the moral point is made. On the Mississippi riverboat the *Fidèle*:

> Natives of all sorts, and foreigners; men of business and men of pleasure; parlor men and backwoodsmen; farmhunters and fame-hunters; heiress hunters, gold-hunters, buffalo-hunters, . . . and hunters after all these hunters. Fine ladies in slippers and moccasined squaws; Northern speculators and Eastern philosophers; English, Irish,

German, Scotch, Danes; Sante Fe traders in striped blankets; and Broadway bucks in cravats of cloth of gold; fine-looking Kentucky boatman, and Japanese looking Mississippi cotton-planters; Quakers in full drab, and United States soldiers in full regimentals; slaves, black, mulatto, quadroon; modish young Spanish Creoles, and old-fashioned French Jews; Mormons and Papists. . . .

A pale deaf-mute urging Scriptural charity, a crippled black beggar, the Man with the Weed in putative mourning, make their appearance to be transformed into an agent of the Black Rapids Coal Company with valuable shares to sell at a reduction; to pose as the inventor of the Protean easy chair, the Omni-Balsamic Reinvigorator; the agent of the widow and orphan asylum "recently founded among the Seminoles"; the promoter of a real-estate venture called the New Jerusalem. On and on the masquerades and scams breeze over the *Fidèle,* one more outrageous than another and each to meet a passenger-victim described with prejudices and hidden desires useful to the swindlers. The exchanges between the victims and the imaginative thieves are little dramas of sly conviction.

The English reviews of the book were more favorable than the American, perhaps because they were not unhappy with a text that portrays "the money-getting spirit which appears to pervade every class of men in the States, almost like a monomania." The American press recognized the cleverness but often lamented the metaphysical and discursive nature of the composition along with the stress upon the disreputable band of citizens of the Republic.

Among the most imaginative later critics in Melville's unending bibliography, there has been much dissatisfaction. Newton Arvin wrote in the 1950s that *The Confidence-Man* was, of all Melville's novels, "the dreariest, most unbelieving." Daniel Hoffman, in an interesting essay, found that "the satiric power of individual episodes and characters—was won at the cost of a larger failure." F. O. Matthiessen: "The discrepancy between what Melville said was to be found on the Mississippi and the bleak sense of existence that he managed to create there would suggest that he had no adequate grasp of this kind of society."

As we read today, every year brings a demolition of the shape long ordained for short stories, the novel, and poetry. *The Confidence-Man,* in the liberty it takes to go where it will on its own terms, to digress, to introduce and abandon themes in an anarchic restlessness, *becomes* a modern novel. The wild expansiveness of the economy in the middle 1800s, the Melville family's ranging inability to profit, the exaggerated patriotic claims of the country, give a sharp kind of pseudorealism to the incidents in the fiction. It is an enclosed idea, fertile in illustration of the reigning notion; its roguish pessimism is a sigh for self-serving credulity rather than an isolating indignation. Indeed, who could wish Melville not to have written this *comedie noir,* his text before signing off from the fiction market—or lack of a market?

Hawthorne

THE LETTER OF APPRECIATION Hawthorne wrote to Melville after he had received a copy of *Moby-Dick,* "dedicated to his genius," has not survived Melville's trash can or open fire. The letter is a loss because the high approval led Melville to believe that a kind of apostolic union existed between the two. His language in reply is extravagant but quite moving: "I feel the Godhead is broken up like the bread at the Supper, and that we are the pieces. Hence this infinite fraternity of feeling." Perhaps Hawthorne was taken aback by the intensity, so unlike his own reserve; perhaps he had not meant to share the mantle of genius with his younger contemporary. In any case, American literature came to agree with the assumption into heaven of the two writers, however belatedly for the faithful, obscure miracle worker Melville. The Hawthornes left the Berkshires for Concord, and this led to a normal gap in the relationship. And yet Melville retained a feeling of deep, if obscure, hurt, and there is much that is ghostly in the collision.

Hawthorne, or so it is thought, appears in the long poem *Clarel,* which Melville wrote twenty years after he

visited the family in England. Hawthorne himself had
been dead for twelve years, but the puzzle of his nature
was still sadly alive to Melville, a kind of wounding beyond the grave. In the poem, set in the Holy Land, a
gifted, distinguished American by the name of Vine is
among those sojourning in the old Biblical places. It is
young Clarel, a theological student, who will try to con-
quer the attention of Vine (Hawthorne). Vine appears in a
canto titled "The Recluse," and he is odd in his own fashion. Manner shy; a lack of "parlor-wont." He had no trace
of "passion's soul or lucre's stain," although his life is half
over. A subtle virtue he has, "but evinced no nature saintly
fine"; instead, "under cheer of opulent softness, reigned
austere control of self."

The impudent, heart-sore portrait continues; "desire
mortified" but less from morality than from doubt happi-
ness is possible. Old Vine prized the beauty of the world
"tho it scarce might warm." Vine is then compared to a
nun whose "virgin soul communed with men but thro' the
wicket." Shade and fear have chilled Vine's heart even as
they may be said to have enriched his art.

In Gethsemane, site of the Passion, a now enraptured
Clarel finds Vine reading the Scriptures. When, as a flirtatious entrée, he asks the preoccupied man to read aloud,
he is met with a stare, "absent and wildered, vacant there."
Clarel, an intrusive nuisance asking for a florid intimacy
with the indifferent Vine, is a poor substitute for the yearning Melville, but the lines stand for the betrayed hopes of
the days and nights in Pittsfield.

Ah, clear sweet ether of the soul
(Mused Clarel), holding him in view.
Prior advances unreturned
Not here he recked of, while he yearned—
O, now but for communion true
And close; let go each alien theme;
Give me thyself!

The Scarlet Letter was published in 1850; *Moby-Dick,* in 1851. Hawthorne's masterpiece established him as a major star in American literature; Melville's masterpiece dimmed and faded away. Chagrin on Melville's part, despite his admiration for Hawthorne's talent, is always possible in this stinging obsession, but it would seem the chagrin lies in personal inequality of affection. What Clarel, in the poem, could have wished from Hawthorne is murky and psychologically peculiar. "Give me thyself!" The yearning, regret, and anger endured for a lifetime in its one-sided shape, like an abortive romance in youth troubling the dreams of the rejected one in old age—a condition more often found in sentimental fiction than in life.

On October 11, 1856, Melville shipped out as a passenger on a ship bound for Glasgow. His condition of instability had been so acute that the family persuaded Judge Shaw to finance an extended journey abroad to England, Greece, Italy, and the Holy Land. Hawthorne was the consul in Liverpool, and when Melville arrived, he was shown every courtesy and cordiality, also invited to spend some days with the family in Southport, a seaside resort. Hawthorne noted the visit in his journal, and the passages show a concern and sympathy for Melville he may not have been aware of. In the first item, Melville turns up like a wandering student, shabby and quite bereft of the ludicrous trunks respectable Americans lugged about on the Grand Tour. "He arrived in Southport with the least little bit of a bundle, which, he told me, contained a night shirt and a tooth-brush. He is a person of very gentlemanly instincts in every respect, save that he is a little heterodox in the matter of clean linen."

There is a more haunting notation in Hawthorne's journal, indeed one that will haunt Melville studies very much in the manner of a confession overheard in prison and passed on to the authorities.

. . . on the intervening day, we took a pretty long walk together, and sat down in a hollow among the sand hills . . . and smoked a cigar. Melville, as he always does, began to reason of Providence and futurity, and of everything that lies beyond human ken, and informed me that he had "pretty much made up his mind to be annihilated;" but still he does not seem to rest in that anticipation; and, I think, will never rest until he gets hold of a definite belief. It is strange how he persists—and had persisted ever since I knew him, and probably long before—in wandering to and fro over these deserts, as dismal and monotonous as the sand hills amid which we were sitting. He can neither believe, nor be comfortable in his unbelief; and he is too honest and courageous not to try to do one or the other. If he were a religious man, he would be one of the most truly religious and reverential; he has a very high and noble nature, and better worth of immortality than most of us.

Melville also kept a journal during the months abroad, and there is much of interest in them; however, in the light of the kindly scrutiny Hawthorne cast upon his fellow American, Melville's curt entries about the visit are unexceptional:

> Saw Mr. Hawthorne at the Consulate. Invited me to stay with him during my sojourn in Liverpool.
> Took a long walk by the sea . . . Good talk . . . Mrs. Hawthorne not in good health. Mr. H. stayed home with me.
> Mr. H and I took the train for Liverpool. Spent rest of the day pressing inquiries among steamers, . . . etc.

Hawthorne's fateful notations about Melville's wandering discussions on religion seem to indicate a sobering maturity for the pagan iconoclast. Melville was born into the Dutch Reform Church of the Gansevoort family, and thus "his" church was that of the mother, as such matters are conventionally ordered. However, his father, Allan Melville, was a Unitarian, the relaxed doctrinal preference of many Bostonians, including the Shaws. Melville was married in the Unitarian Church, wives having precedence here, as mothers have in baptisms.

The Calvinist roots of the Dutch Reform Church, modified in America in the eighteenth and nineteenth centuries, are thought to have left their mark on the son of Maria Gansevoort. However, insofar as the Melville household is concerned, biographies do not find the family forever at prayer, enduring a pious and meekly reverent life like that described by Sir Edmund Gosse about his evangelical parents. Augusta, Melville's sister, seems to have been churchly, but that does not appear dominant with his brothers Gansevoort and Allan. One thing is certain: Maria Melville had nothing to teach Herman about the innate depravity of mankind.

Maria Melville appears most of all to be conventional, worried and mindful of appearance, proud and snobbish. She is dominating, bossy, perhaps going to church with a social sense of belonging and respectability as much as with clerical conviction. The Gansevoort family in Albany was prosperous and respectable, but Maria's generation does not appear to be overwhelmed by Calvinism and fear of damnation. Two of Melville's Gansevoort cousins were victims of the flesh—alcoholism and syphilis. What Maria wanted for her family was worldly success. For some Calvinists success was a sign of election, but it is agreeable in itself. Still, a mother is a mother, a birthmark inexpungable, but this mother gives little indication of having spiritual or intellectual power over her brilliant son.

Herman Melville came to his metaphysical puzzling by way of his own restless curiosity. When, with Hawthorne, he was wandering to and fro over the dismal deserts of theology, Biblical criticism and anthropology were enlightening and troubling the intellectual landscape. Hawthorne knew the struggle of the heart in the battle with the real dimensions of a lived life, but he was not so disputatious as Melville, perhaps not so personalized in his confrontations with abstractions such as the terms of Christian belief. His notion that Melville could benefit from coming to belief is an idle wish Melville's defiant nature could not easily honor. And so "he had made up his mind to be annihilated"—a rejection of the Resurrection and life eternal?

In *Moby-Dick,* Melville goes to the Whaleman's Chapel and there sees the inscriptions of the tablets dedicated to those who died at sea, an unconsecrated death. He wonders, "How it is that we refuse to be comforted for those who we nevertheless maintain are dwelling in unspeakable bliss?" And he adds in an opaque but beautiful line: "Faith, like a jackal, feeds among the tombs, and even from these dead doubts she gathers her most vital hope." The poetry of a doubting soul who knew the engulfing finality of a death at sea.

A mind like Melville's, certainly skeptical if not atheistic, is more troubled by God than the perfunctory, dozing churchgoer. For Melville, God's world is a place of injustice, suffering, war, and starvation. But there it is: The lack of God's ameliorating hand is unbearable to many and is relieved in the world's religions by superstitions that give hope or resignation. Apostasy is a philosophical and metaphysical burden; it is lonely, a scorn of the millions who, when the census taker comes around, insist they believe in God and, if of the Christian faith, in eternal life through the martyrdom and resurrection of Jesus Christ. As St. Paul wrote, without the Resurrection your faith is nothing. If Melville was wandering to and fro on the serious religious questions of the day, it need not mean he was "tortured" by the remnants of the Dutch Reform Church taken in at his mother's knee. As an intellectual, friendless except for books, Melville detested superstitions and meddling missionaries. He accepts, as he must, "annihilation." Critics, noting the lonely study of the philosophical questions of the mid-nineteenth century, are too quick to rob him of a melancholy atheism, the moral intransigence of one acquainted with those damned by life.

Twenty years after returning from his six months abroad, he wrote and published a poem about the Holy Land and here and there about Hawthorne. *Clarel*–some eighteen thousand lines. When Carlyle was slaving over his biography of Frederick the Great, his wife said, "Would Frederick had died as a baby." About *Clarel,* one is tempted to say: Would the winds had swept the ship past the port of Jaffa in Palestine. *Clarel* is a sort of verse novel, with many characters representing contemporary positions about theological questions of faith and doubt. Clarel, of the title, is a young American theological student, somewhat wooden, a post against which are flung the opinions of more volatile pilgrims.

Palestine in antiquity was a stone-strewn land, long geologically helpless in its natural configuration. For the travelers of the 1850s, born into the cult of the Holy Places, with their resonant sanctification, the harsh soil is a down-dropping disappointment. Melville's journal about Jerusalem and spots nearby is a dirge of stony greyness, darkness, and dust. The Holy Sepulchre: "Nearby is a blind stair of worn marble, ascending to the reputed Calvary . . . the hole in which the cross was fixed . . . as over a cole-cellar." The whole city of Jerusalem is "grey & looks at you like a cold grey eye in a cold old man." "In the emptiness of the lifeless antiquity of Jerusalem the emigrant Jews are like flies that have taken up their abode in a skull."

Judea: a tornado of stones, "stony mountains & stony plains; stony torrents & stony roads; stony walls & stony fields, stony houses & stony tombs . . . " Attended a missionary meeting in Jerusalem (to raise money for some other faraway place) "but was not specially edified."

Melville and his inclination to obsessive themes can, in the matter of Hawthorne, be laid at the foot of the altar of art; "two pieces of the Godhead" they were to be, and yet the consummation went asunder.

Obsession and a compulsive need for *confession;* homoerotic intrusions came into his writing again and again with an unknown intention; subliminal matter, unconscious or boldly aware? Perhaps he is as blind as his readers, unacquainted with the naming of irregular impulses. Love scenes on the beach of his fiction lay undisturbed like any other specimen of conchology. Later readers picked up the bright shells with the avidity of collectors and would find that the crinkles and striations once held a secret, troubled heart.

Sophia Hawthorne read *Moby-Dick,* as we learn from that letter-saving couple by the way of Melville's reply to her.

> It really amazed me that you should find any satisfaction in the book. It is true that some *men* have said they were pleased with it, but you are the only *woman* . . . your allusion for example to the "spirit Spout" first showed me that there are subtle significance in that thing—but I did not, in that case, *mean* it.

The "spirit Spout" chapter, washed in a silvery moonlight, a silvery silence, is a hymn to the silvery jet of a whale coming up for air under a celestial moon, "like some plumed and glittering god uprising from the sea." Whales are not hunted at night for the obvious reason of difficulty and danger to the hunters. But this midnight jet, seen from the mainmast by the sinister Fedallah, is one of the many pauses in Melville's recollection that bring forth passages of lambent, caressing beauty. The midnight foam, with its metallic luster, might indeed foretell of the looming presence of the White Whale luring the "ivory-tusked" *Pequod* to its doom.

Hawthorne read *Moby-Dick.* Sophia Hawthorne, by citing a particular passage, did more than a wifely scanning of the difficult novel; the pages were known by Elizabeth

Melville and perhaps his sister Augusta, the faithful copyists. It was read by publishers, reviewers, the public, many of whom had encountered the friendship of Redburn and the daunting ephebe Harry Bolton. In the 1840s and 1850s we find an innocence or a blindness in what is now a more aggressive and suspicious eye upon a page. When Melville was unearthed like a cryptic finding in a long-hidden desert, the suggestiveness of some encounters came to be seen as acute strains of "homoeroticism"; the sweetness and amiability of the emotions noted to be in contrast to the cynical flashings about marriage. "By heaven, but marriage is an impious thing!"

Ishmael, young, white, with the shadings of irregularity and social bastardy that attach to his name, is, nevertheless, from an "old established family"; he has been a schoolmaster; he is, or has been, Herman Melville, now setting out as a common sailor. He arrives in New Bedford to await several days later the passage to Nantucket, where the *Pequod* will be launched. There, for want of a separate accommodation, he will spend his time in the Spouter-Inn, where he must share a capacious bed with the dark, tattooed harpooner Queequeg. Melville might have described the fate that sent him such an outlandish companion as a picturesque interlude. Instead, what he gave Sophia Peabody to read was altogether startling, although she does not appear to have been startled.

The nights at the Spouter-Inn, by way of a cloudburst of matrimonial images, are offered with a pleasant and sentimental assurance. Preceding the evening retiring, every barrier to sexual attraction between the two has been carefully outlined. Before returning to the inn, we learn that Queequeg has been wandering about town trying to sell a shrunken head, negotiable loot from his voyages, although the innkeeper says the market is now overloaded. When the bedmate at last appears, he is tattooed from head to foot; his face is dark, purplish, yellow; no hair on his head except for a small scalp knot. He smokes from a diabolical instrument shaped like a tomahawk and goes about his nocturnal affairs by obeisance to a little heathen black Congo icon. It will turn out that he shaves with his deadly sharp harpoon.

In the morning, Ishmael awakens to find the pagan arm thrown across him. He tries to unlock the "bridegroom grasp," only to be "hugged tight." The following day is Sunday, and they are off to the chapel and to Father Mapple's Jonah sermon. Back at the inn, Queequeg is quiet and reserved, causing Ishmael to be chagrined after the previous show of affection. In a kind of jealousy and disappointment, he studies the countenance of the primitive and decides that in his dignity and composure Queequeg reminds him of George Washington, "cannibalistically developed."

Ishmael, in the manner of a pursuer, will share a smoke even though he had protested the infamous cloud when they first met. Queequeg at last inquires if they are to be again bedfellows, and when the answer is yes, "he pressed his forehead against mine, clasped me around the waist, and said that hence forth we were married; meaning in his country's phrase, that we were bosom friends." The union is further cemented by Ishmael's making a symbolic religious conversion such as couples from different faiths or denominations may do as a mark of respect and love commitment.

"I was a good Christian; born and bred in the bosom of the infallible Presbyterian Church." With Queequeg he must turn idolater and so kisses the little wooden idol, salaamed before him, and the two went off to sleep, "but not before a little chat."

> How it is I know not; but there is no place like a bed for confidential disclosures between friends. Man and wife, they say, there open the very bottom of their souls to each other, and some couples often lie and chat over old times till early morning. Thus, then, in our heart's honeymoon, lay I and Queequeg—a cozy, loving couple.

Aboard the vessel from New Bedford to Nantucket, Queequeg will show himself worthy of love. The passengers took note of the unusual companionship between the two, and one "bumpkin" who had insulted the "cannibal" was picked up by Queequeg and thrown into the air. When later the offending one fell overboard, it was the powerful Queequeg who dived into the freezing foam and rescued him.

As the narration shifts to the *Pequod,* Ishmael and Queequeg will be separated by function and by the domination in the narrative of Ahab, Starbuck, the mates, the stowaways, and finally the chase, with its funereal conclusion. However, the subterranean betrothal will not be broken. Deep into the narrative, Ishmael and Queequeg take part in the "cutting in" of a captured whale, and here they are tied together by a monkey rope as they proceed in dangerous, slippery work on the back of the whale. The rope will resurrect the marital tie.

> So that for better or for worse, we two, for the time, were wedded; and should poor Queequeg sink to rise no more, then both usage and honor demanded, that instead of cutting the cord, it should drag me down in his wake. So, then, an elongated Siamese ligature united us. Queequeg was my own inseparable twin brother.

In the chapter "A Squeeze of the Hand," and in "The Cassock," refined or nervous sensibilities were challenged with a ferocious bravado. Ishmael's celebration of his hands in the huge tubs of whale sperm, soothing as it is, is also an extraordinary excitation, a sinking or rising into description of fantastical pleasure, and an inadvertent union with the other sailors. "I squeezed that sperm till a strange sort of insanity came over me; and I found myself unwittingly squeezing my co-laborers' hands in it, mistaking their hands for gentle globules."

Abounding feelings of the ultimate felicity, paradise. Paradise, he remembers, is ordained by custom to rest in the wife, the country, and so on. But in his visions: "I saw long rows of angels in paradise, each with his hands in a jar of spermaceti." The very short chapter "The Cassock" is about a "garment" made from the huge, stretched foreskin of the whale. Stretched and dried by the ship's "mincer," it becomes large enough for him to wear it as a "canonical" cloak. And there is the man "arrayed in decent black; occupying a conspicuous pulpit, . . . what a candidate for an archbishopric, what a lad for a Pope were this mincer!" The whale, any whale, is immensely masculine, and getting close to the outrage or sublimity of the body arouses pornographic dreams in the puny little sailors with their spears. Or perhaps Melville meant the foreskin and its infamous domestication into a vestment to be just more information about the habits of the whalemen, the enterprise, sociology, anatomy, commercial labor, to bring oil for the lamps of America. Even as he was writing in 1851, the decline of the New England whaling industry was on the horizon. Still, the cassock was not likely to appear on the balance sheet in the shipowner's office. The little chapter is in the book a wild impertinence.

The love lyric that opens *Moby-Dick* is composed in practical, homely language different from the gorgeous word intoxication of the rest of the novel. "We will not speak of all Queequeg's peculiarities here; how he eschewed coffee and hot rolls, and applied his undivided attention to beefsteaks, done rare." Quequeeg is given a "simple, honest heart"; he has "a lofty bearing which even his uncouthness could not altogether maim"; pleasant, genial, natural, cozy, loving, sociable, a serene household joy. The pages were largely written in Pittsfield, Massachusetts, where his wife, one son and another to be born, his mother, sisters, were in residence.

Everyone is about except Melville himself, who is

apart, dreaming and remembering in the depths of *Moby-Dick* a violent submersion near to drowning. Experience of the sea, the whalers, magnified by research volumes duly tracked down by scholars, but the *Pequod* did not sail from Nantucket or elsewhere with Queequeg, harpooner, noted in the log. *Moby-Dick* is the imagination's release from actual boats and islands, from Toby and Long John Ghost and Jack Chase. We are told Melville was in ill health, depressed, but in these mornings alone he is in an elation of freedom and passion. As the final words come into view, Ishmael alone drifts to safety in what began as the savage's coffin and became the lifesaving raft, the floating bed of the cozy, loving pair. All the knots are tied.

And then, it is unsettling to have Ishmael in Pittsfield coming down to dinner at night where the talk will be of money. More dislocating to find him retiring to the bedchamber to produce, after Malcolm and Stanwix, his daughters, Elizabeth and Frances. The assembled family cannot have had any idea of this reluctant head of the household. Nor can the graduate students with their theses, the annotators, the eyes searching passages marked in his books, the critics, the biographers in long, long efforts and short ones. It must be said about Melville that he earned the mystery of his inner life.

In the illicit proddings undertaken herein, *Redburn*, the book and the young man so named, the first voyage, have the tone of autobiography and are indeed more intimate than the memory of the deserter in *Typee, Omoo* and *White-Jacket*. On the merchant ship *St. Lawrence*, Melville is twenty years old and engaged to do service to Liverpool and back for a period of four months. When the boat is in the harbor and the crew is free to roam the city, he encounters a young man named Harry Bolton.

Harry Bolton is lifelike as a certain type of frenzied, melodramatic young homosexual down on his luck, and as such he is as embarrassing and interesting as life itself. Redburn, that is, Melville, is both accepting and suspicious of Harry, but there is everything about the encounter as told that seems to reveal a striking innocence of heart and mind or defiance in offering the scenes to the public. Nothing in the early parts of the novel would lead us to anticipate the extravagant, interesting, sudden drive into a richly decorated underworld.

The two meet on the streets of Liverpool, and Redburn is immediately attracted. Harry is not a dumb, deadened fish in the human pool of the seamen. He is a stranger, an English youth, fluent in self-creation.

A street meeting with a "handsome, accomplished, but unfortunate youth." Small, with the perfectly formed legs, curling hair, silken muscles, complexion feminine as a girl's; eyes large, black and womanly, voice like a harp; and difficult to imagine how this "delicate exotic from the conservatories of some Regent street" came to the potato patches of Liverpool. In a bar, Harry will be chatting about the possibility of going to America, and thus the friendship with this "incontrovertible son of a gentleman" began. Harry will tell his story; born in the old city of Bury, orphaned but heir to a fortune of a thousand pounds. Off to the city, where with gambling sportsmen and dandies fortune lost to the last sovereign.

More elaboration from the new friend: embarked for Bombay as a midshipman in the East India Service, claimed to have handled the masts, and was taken on board Redburn's ship, which was not due to leave for a few days. Together in the roadside inns, every fascination—more news about the companion and his friendship with the Marquis of Waterford and Lady Georgiana Theresa, the noble daughter of an anonymous earl.

Harry is stone-broke one moment but darts away and will return with money that will provide for an astonishing trip to London. (There is no record of a trip from Liverpool to London during this early journey in 1839 or by the time the book was published in 1849, when Melville sailed to London for the first time almost two weeks after the publication of *Redburn*.) When they alight in the city, Harry puts on a mustache and whiskers as a "precaution against being recognized by particular friends in London." A feverish atmosphere of hysteria and panic falls upon poor Harry and is part of the chiaroscuro mastery with which his character and the club scene that follows are so brilliantly rendered. And fearlessly rendered in sexual images of decadence and privilege in an astonishing embrace.

The club is a "semi-public place of opulent entertainment" described in a mixture of subterranean images—Paris catacombs—and *faux* Farnese palace decorations. In the first room entered there is a fresco ceiling of elaborate detail. Under the gaslights it seems to the bewildered gaze of Redburn to have the glow of the "moon-lit garden of Porcia at Belmont; and the gentle lovers, Lorenzo and Jes-

sica, lurked somewhere among the vines." There are obsequious waiters dashing about, under the direction of an
old man "with snow-white hair and whiskers, and in a
snow-white jacket—he looked like an almond tree in blos-
som. . . ." In a conventional club manner, there are knots
of gentlemen "with cut-glass decanters and taper-waisted
glasses, journals and cigars, before them."

Redburn, throughout the scene, is curious and alarmed
by Harry's way of leaving him standing alone in this unaccountable atmosphere. They proceed to a more private
room; so thick were the Persian carpets that he feels he is
sinking into "some reluctant, sedgy sea." Oriental ot-
tomans "wrought into plaited serpents" and "such pictures
as Martial and Suetonius mention as being found in the
private cabinet of the Emperor Tiberius." A bust of an old
man with a "mysteriously wicked expression, and impos-
ing silence by one thin finger over his lips. His marble
mouth seemed tremulous with secrets."

Harry, in a frantic return to private business, suddenly
puts a letter into Redburn's hand, which he is to post if
Harry does not return by morning. And off he goes, but
not before introducing Redburn to the attendant as young
Lord Stormont. To the now terrified American, penniless
son of a senator and so on, the place seemed "infected,"
as if some "eastern plague had been imported." The door
will partly open, and there will be a "tall, frantic man, with
clenched hands, wildly darting through the passage,
toward the stairs." On Redburn goes in images of fear
and revulsion. "All the mirrors and marbles around me
seemed crawling with lizards, and I thought to myself, that

though gilded and golden, the serpent of vice is a serpent still."

The macabre excursion, with its slithering images, passes as in a tormented dream, and Harry returns to say, "I'm off to America. The game is up."

The relation between the two resumes its boyish pleasantries. Back on ship, Harry, in full maquillage, comes on deck in a "brocaded dressing-gown, embroidered slippers, and tasseled smoking-cap, to stand his morning watch." When ordered to climb the rigging, he falls into a faint, and it became clear that his account of shipping to Bombay was another handy fabrication. Nevertheless, Redburn remains faithful in friendship, and landing in New York, the chapter heading is *"Redburn and Harry, Arm and Arm, in Harbor."* Redburn shows him around, introduces him to a friend in the hope of finding work, and then leaves him, as he must, since he could hardly take the swain back to Lansingburgh. Years later he will learn that Harry Bolton had signed on another ship and fallen or jumped overboard.

In the novel there is another encounter, this of lyrical enthusiasm untainted by the London infested underworld. It is Carlo, "with thick clusters of tendril curls, half overhanging the brows and delicate ears." His "naked leg was beautiful to behold as any lady's arm, so soft and rounded, with infantile ease and grace." He goes through life playing his hand organ in the streets for coins. Now, on the deck, Redburn sinks into a paroxysm of joy at the sound of the "humble" music:

Play on, play on, Italian boy! Turn hither your positive, morning eyes . . . let me gaze fathoms down into thy fathomless eye. . . . All this could Carlo do—make, unmake me; and join me limb to limb . . . And Carlo! ill betide the voice that ever greets thee, my Italian boy, with aught but kindness; cursed the slave who ever drives thy wondrous box of sights and sounds forth from a lordling's door!

The scenes with Harry Bolton were not much admired; as an "intrusion," contemporary critics seemed to rebuke them for structural defects rather than for the efflorescent adjectives, the swooning intimacy of feeling for male beauty of a classical androgynous perfection that will reach its transcendence in the innocent loveliness of Billy Budd, Melville's heartbreaking, deathbed vision.

Hershel Parker, the encyclopedic biographer and tireless Melville scholar, finds no charm in the "flaccid" Harry Bolton and has interesting thoughts on why Melville was so clearly dismissive of *Redburn,* a work of enduring interest. "What he thought he was doing in it, as a young married man and a new father, is an unanswered question." And: " . . . only a young and still naïve man could have thought he could write a kind of psychological autobiography . . . without suffering any consequences." Parker suggests that Melville came to understand the folly of what he had written, came to acknowledge that he had revealed homosexual longings or even homosexual experience.

Parker provides another item in the atmosphere that surrounded the days and nights of the writer. At the time, there sprang up in America a group called the Come-Outers, a sect wishing to follow Paul's exhortation in 2 Corinthians 6:17. "Wherefore come out from them, and be ye separate." It was the object of the group to reveal information ordinarily held private. Parker's research seems to indicate that Melville knew about the sect but did not notice that he had "unwittingly joined the psychological equivalent of this new American religious sect; in mythological terms, he had opened Pandora's box when he thought he was merely describing the lid."

It is not clear whether the Come-Outers were, as in the present use of the term, to announce themselves as homosexual when such revelations were relevant. In the Biblical text, Paul seems to be referring to Corinthians who were worshiping idols or pretending to virtues they did not practice, such as sorrow while rejoicing, pretending poverty while piling up riches.

However, if Melville rejected *Redburn* because he came to see it as an embarrassing and unworthy self-revelation, why did he in the subsequent *Moby-Dick* create the tender union of Queequeg and Ishmael? Another wonder about life and art: Where did Melville come upon the ornate and lascivious men's club described with feral acuteness in *Redburn?* There is no record unearthed like the cinders and ashes of Pompeii to bring the night journey into history. But does the blank forever erase the possibility that the diversion actually took place? Harder to credit that

Melville in his imagination, or from what is sometimes called his use and abuse of sources, was altogether free of the lush, disorienting opening of doors.

The presence of delicate, hardly seaworthy, men, some in officer positions on the rigorous, hierarchical sailing vessels, is an occupational puzzle that has the accent of reportage, or at least of plausibility. The frail Captain Guy, already mentioned in *Omoo;* Selvagee in *White-Jacket,* with his cologne baths, lace-bordered handkerchiefs, cravats, and curling irons, although an inept sailor, is a Lieutenant on a U.S. naval ship.

Jack Chase, the educated, manly friend in *White-Jacket* to whom *Billy Budd* was dedicated some forty-seven years later, may have been a romantic attachment for Melville's unsteady emotions. Chase is a man of the world, and yet he ships as a common seaman due to refusal to accept unearned authority. He is by wish something of a misfit who might have thrived on land or sea but will have it otherwise as an expression of a strong but wayward character. He drinks and wanders the earth as he will, a brave seaman of the foretop. "Wherever you may now be rolling over the blue billows, dear Jack! take my best love along with you; and God bless you, wherever you go." The same sense of a lost wanderer illuminates the dedication in *Billy Budd:* To Jack Chase Englishman: "Wherever that great heart may be. Here on Earth or harbored in Paradise.

The perfumed mates on shipboard are mildly made fun of. The beautiful Harry Bolton, the lying, street-smart, and thoroughly disreputable companion, is understood by Melville, or by young Redburn, in all his foolish disarray, and yet they will end up arm in arm on the streets of New York; but it is only with Queequeg that there is bodily closeness—Queequeg, homely son of a High Chief with the "cannibal propensity he nourished in his untutored youth."

After his few years at sea in his twenties, Melville lived among decent, well-bred men and women, all the while knowing much of life they could not have known. Reading his books did not seem to beam the rays of his deep remoteness any more than if he had been writing about time spent with Indians in the Plains. Hawthorne, over the dangerous brandy and cigars late at night, may have sensed, if not named or understood, the cleavage in Melville's nature and sensibility. In his review of *Typee* before their meeting, he had noted that the author had "that freedom of view—it would be too harsh to call it laxity of principle—which renders him tolerant of codes of morals that may be little in accordance with our own," adding that such would be proper to the circumstances in the book. Later, the exuberance of Melville, upon coming into an intellectual and creative friendship with a fellow writer, could bring alarm. "Give me thyself!" was there in the late firelight from the beginning.

The biographer Ms. Robertson-Lorant, in addition to noting that Melville's son Stanwix died with a male friend at his bedside, writes of Melville's attempt in *Redburn* to come to terms with sexuality—and to this she adds a teasing clause: "or perhaps to come to terms with something only he knew about his older brother. Does Harry represent something troubling about Gansevoort?" We seem by unanswered questions to be in a cemetery of remains with uneasy genetic secrets. But then, so much about Melville is *seems to be, may have been,* and *perhaps.*

Billy Budd

*BILLY BUDD, FORETOPMAN,** left at death in an unfinished or unedited state and preserved by his wife. A return to prose fiction, a last will and testament, a going back to the spirit of his earlier work, before the diversion into poetry. He is ailing, plagued, as he has been forever, by trouble with his eyes, and yet the luminous imagination remains with this strange man as if reluctant to be blotted out by darkness. In *Billy Budd* he writes a lyrical tragedy on the extremes in human character, a contemplation of goodness appearing as naturally as a sunrise and of midnight evil also inhabiting a human soul naturally, without necessity or even clear advantage.

Into this deeply affecting reflection on the human condition, he has imagined details of a challenging singular-

---

*Scholars, deciphering the messy manuscript, have decided that Melville's final title was *Billy Budd, Sailor.* I have kept *Foretopman* out of a sentimental affection for the old title under which most of us first read the story. The name of the ship, formerly the *Indomitable,* was changed by Melville to the *Bellipotent,* and I have reluctantly honored that. Still, it's hard to imagine that the ribald old sailors would have wished to sign on the "Belly-potent."

ity; and as a storyteller there is a magical plot, a dramatic series of actions, without which the tale would be a philosophical daydream. Billy Budd, a young sailor of preternatural beauty, good nature, and loyalty, is accused by the master-at-arms, a sort of naval MP, of intention to mutiny. The young sailor, who, under stress, suffers from a stutter or speech pause, is unable to express his innocence and outrage and strikes out at the accuser, killing him by a blow. According to maritime law, the sailor, Billy Budd, must be hanged and his body consigned to the sea.

But who is Billy Budd? He is a curiosity indeed, almost defying credible description. He is the Handsome Sailor, he is Apollo with a portmanteau, he is Baby Budd, he is Beauty—all of these things as he comes swinging onto the English ship the *Bellipotent*. He is twenty-one, an able-bodied seaman, fit to climb the great sails, as if ready to fly. Billy is also from the first a creature of inborn moral sweetness. He is free and innocent, a beautiful changeling from nowhere. In fact, he is an orphan, an illiterate, reminding one of a freshly hatched, brilliantly colored bird. His only flaw is the one mentioned, the stutter under stress. Peaceful himself, he brings peace to those around him "like a Catholic priest striking peace in an Irish shindy."

Melville gives evidence of a compositional strain to bring credibility to the beloved youth, to the demands of his perfection, united with the purest naturalness. The pictorial Billy: "A lingering adolescent expression in the as yet smooth face, all but feminine in purity of natural complexion." And then a leap: "Cast in a mold peculiar to the finest physical examples of those Englishmen in whom the

Saxon strain would seem not at all to partake of any Norman or other admixture, he showed in his face that humane look of reposeful good nature which the Greek sculptor in some instances gave to the heroic strong man, Hercules." The pretty boy as Hercules is a preparation for the development of the story. The captain of the ship from which Billy was taken, impressed, by the *Bellipotent* told of an altercation on his ship in which Billy had been insulted by a sailor named Red Whiskers. "Quick as lightning Billy let fly his arm. I dare say he never meant to do as much as he did, but anyhow he gave the burly fool a terrible drubbing." Billy's previous ship was named *Rights-of-Man*.

John Claggart, the Master-at-Arms, is a mirror opposite of Billy Budd. His unaccountable but concentrated hostility to the universally loved Billy is a conundrum, an exceptional circumstance. Claggart exhibits the floating, "motiveless malignity" Coleridge in a kind of psychological resignation falls back on as the explanation for Shakespeare's Iago. Like Billy, Claggart has no known past, no baggage of previous circumstance to carry about with him. He has entered the naval ship at thirty-five, causing his shipmates to imagine some cloud of disrepute driving him.

He is carefully described by Melville, the lover of verbal portraiture. Claggart does not cut an ill figure, being spare and tall, with clean-cut features, except that something about his chin recalls the Titus Oates of the Popish plot. It is noted that Claggart's hands do not give evidence of hard toil, and his complexion is interestingly pale for a seaman. He is educated, and there is something in his speech not quite that of a native-born Englishman. However he entered the man-of-war's crew, Claggart soon made his mark due to "the superior capacity he immediately evinced, his constitutional sobriety, and ingratiating deference to superiors, together with a peculiar ferreting genius manifested on a singular occasion; all this, capped by a certain austere patriotism, abruptly advanced him to the position of master-at-arms."

Claggart will take a bold dislike for Billy Budd that will infect his spirit with an inflammatory passion, outwardly controlled by the "uncommon prudence" habitual with "the subtler depravity." And, as such natures can, Claggart enlists the help of a corrupt, sniveling crewman called Squeak, who tries to enlist Billy Budd, an impressed seaman, into thoughts of mutiny but is violently rejected by the Hercules in Billy's nature.

And yet another coil in Claggart's twisted nature:

When Claggart's unobserved glance happened to light on belted Billy rolling along the upper gun deck in the leisure of the second dogwatch . . . that glance would follow the cheerful sea Hyperion with a settled meditative and melancholy expression, his eyes strangely suffused with incipient feverish tears. Then would Claggart look like a man of sorrows. Yes, and sometimes the melancholy expression would have in it a touch of soft yearning, as if Claggart could even have loved Billy but for fate and ban.

Thinking about the dense stabs in the thicket of Claggart's character, the great American critic F. O. Matthiesen writes: ". . . a writer today would be fully aware of what may have been only latent for Melville, the sexual element in Claggart's ambivalence. Even if Melville did not have this consciously in mind, it emerges for the reader now with intense psychological accuracy."

The story is set on British ships in 1797 after the fleet mutiny at Nore. Crews seized a ship previously at Spithead, sent the officers ashore, in protest against the brutal conditions prevailing in the British navy. The mutiny at Nore was a more serious outbreak, a threat to Britain's sea power, and also felt connected to the tide of revolutionary feeling spreading from France and from Napoleon's conquests. The *Bellipotent* has been called to shift from merchant service to a man-of-war. For this purpose, men were dragged off the street and impressed into service, and thus Billy is taken from his ship, *Rights-of-Man*. He is willing to serve, and as he boards his new berth, he cheerfully waves to the departing vessel and calls out, "And good-bye to you, too, old *Rights-of-Man*." This, interpreted, or in pretended interpretation, will figure in the claim by Claggart that Billy is inciting the *Bellipotent* to mutiny.

The accusation is brought to Captain Vere, who summons Billy to a confrontation with Claggart in his quarters. In the cabin, the captain instructs Claggart to "tell this man to his face what you told of him to me." Billy stood like one "impaled and gagged" while the captain calls out, "Speak, man! . . . Speak! Defend yourself!" The terrible speech impediment overcomes him, and "the next instant, quick as the flame from a discharged cannon at night, his right arm shot out, and Claggart dropped to the deck." Struck down by the Angel of God!

Captain Vere, sometimes called Starry Vere, is a rare being but not one of extreme definition, like Billy and Claggart. At the cabin hearing, Billy proclaims his lack of intention to kill Claggart, and some of the officers speak for a mitigation of the penalty, but Captain Vere will insist that intent is not to the issue. With his admirable qualities as a gentleman, Captain Vere was also known to be somewhat pedantic. He believes Billy's account of his state of mind; he is half in love with the Angel of God himself, and it is clear in the end that the death by hanging, ordained by marine law, will bring a greater grief to him than to the officers pointing to some mitigation, although, as officers, not insisting with vehemence.

At the moment of execution, Billy will call out the justly famous, resounding "God bless Captain Vere!" He expires in a sacramental mist:

> At the same moment it chanced that the vapoury fleece hanging low in the East, was shot through with a soft glory as of the fleece of the Lamb of God seen in a mystical vision; and simultaneously therewith, watched by the wedged mass of upturned faces, Billy ascending, took the full rose of the dawn.

And Captain Vere will die from the wounds inflicted by a musket ball, die with the words "Billy Budd, Billy Budd" on his lips.

Garden of Eden before the Fall, sunlit, happy-go-lucky,

blissful ignorance; there lies the brute human temptation to bewilder confidence, to test, like Claggart, the defensive powers of the beguiling, androgynous athlete. And there in the end is Melville voicing the name of the Angel of God in his last creative work before dying. The reader, too, ascends, like Billy, into the vapory fleece of language to honor this beautiful vision.

In 1856, financed by Judge Shaw, Melville was six months abroad. After leaving Hawthorne in Liverpool, he spent time in the voracious consumption of the treasures of Constantinople, Cairo, Greece, Palestine, Rome, Florence, Venice, and Naples. This journey was said to be for his health and certainly for the health of everyone around him. It was a hard time of fleas and punishing walks, but he took in everything the Grand Tour had to display. Streets, palaces, cathedrals, pyramids, mosques, each painting, statue, and campanile and hospitable café.

Upon his return to Pittsfield, no rest for the weary and out of funds. Money, need for employment, sent him to three seasons on the lecture platform. The first invited the audience with "Statues of Rome" to participate in the great chiselings of equestrian monuments and historical busts. Perhaps taking a hint, that was followed by "The South Seas" and "Travel." Robert Frost, a hero of the lecture circuit, said that hell is a half-filled auditorium—and Melville would come to agree. He didn't earn much in the activity profitable to Henry Ward Beecher and Emerson.

To San Francisco and Panama on a clipper ship captained by his younger brother Thomas. For Melville, on land or at home seems to prompt a wish for anything but here. A practical trip to Washington in pursuit of a consular appointment and again failed to impress. He again prepared for appointments with recommendations and everything needed, but perhaps while confronting the powers behind the desk, he himself came forth in the unpromising manner of a young man at the employment office saying, You don't need anyone here, do you?

Meanwhile, his mind had turned to the writing of poetry. Lizzie Melville, in a harmless but never-to-be-unnoted remark, wrote in a letter: "Herman has taken to writing poetry. You need not tell anyone, for you know how such things get around." The effort was not a pastime but an offering by a professional writer to publishers, and when that was not forthcoming, private funds would send the work to readers. Peter Gansevoort, his brother-in-law, provided money for Putnam to publish *Clarel*.

Death

In 1863 the family traded Arrowhead for Allan Melville's house at 104 East Twenty-sixth Street in Manhattan. Years in the countryside have as many chores as beauties. Outside your window there is the late unmown grass as well as the tall New England trees. There is a miserable little stack of logs waiting to be replenished for the baking oven and the winter bedrooms. A garden is a grave, as Emerson said. And so for whatever reasons, the Melvilles settle on Twenty-sixth Street and in the house where Malcolm will commit suicide and his father will abide until a natural death.

The calamitous years of the Civil War affected Melville as deeply as they affected the whole of the nation. On the streets of New York he could see the young recruits marching off to battle and write: "All wars are boyish, and are fought by boys." He was a Unionist, deplored slavery, also deplored the tribal slaughter; and in this mood he composed his torn, conflicted emotions in *Battle-Pieces and Aspects of the War,* published by Harper in 1866. Enthusiasm is alien to his nature, and in "March into Virginia," ending in the first Manassas, he mourns the plight of the young men who go forth "chatting left and laughing right":

> Shall die experienced ere three days are spent—
>> Perish, enlightened by the volleyed glare;
> Or shame survive, and, like to adamant,
>> The throe of Second Manassas share.

In "The Armies of the Wilderness" the same abhorrence of the fratricidal desolation informs the conclusion:

> Long they withhold the roll
>> Of the shroudless dead. It is right;
> Nor yet can we bear the flare
>> Of the funeral light.

Battle-Pieces, more than a hundred verses, considers all the high points of the war: Antietam, Gettysburg, Sherman in Georgia, Shiloh, the surrender at Appomattox, and the scattered elegies for the unknown dead. Bravery and tragedy, a sense of foreboding, an added prose plea for "reasonable consideration of our late enemies." The publication of the book received more disparagement from distinguished Americans than praise here and there. His moderation, sympathy for both sides of the conflict, offended, and one critic called his verse "epileptic."

Here is William Dean Howells writing that the poems lead one to doubt "there has really been a great war, with battles fought by men and bewailed by women: Or is it only that Mr. Melville's inner consciousness has been perturbed, filled with phantasms of enlistments, marches, fights in the air, parenthetic bulletin-boards, and tortured humanity shedding, not words and blood, but words alone?"

The final thought in Daniel Aaron's splendid book on American writers and the Civil War. "By portraying the War as historical tragedy, Melville defied consensus and took one further step toward popular oblivion."

Meter and rhyme betrayed Melville in his poems and crippled the thrilling agility of the leaping adjectives and verbs that dazzle the poetic prose of *Moby-Dick*. Even the early pages of *Typee* show a mastery of sentence rhythms in their documentation and an uncanny gift for the askew word that once netted falls deftly into place. There is the "villainous *footpad* of the seas," the shark; the "*enameled* and softly swelling plains" of the South Seas; and elsewhere, a boat's "*vindictive* bows" [italics added]. In *Moby-Dick,* he swallows Shakespeare, a holy cistern for his overwrought thirst.

The critic James Wood writes of Melville's "ravishment by metaphor" and in an imaginative leap of his own connects the "as if" of metaphor with Melville's going "to and fro" about God. The love embrace in metaphor with an alternative is the soul of skepticism about God, who is Silence. Wood's black-magic brilliance finds that if you "bring God into the sea of metaphor, on equal terms with everything else," you "dare the infidel idea that *God is only a metaphor.*"

Hawthorne's journal notation about Melville's going

to and fro in the dismal sands of theology can also bring to mind Milton's Satan going to and fro in the Garden of Eden, all the while plotting the hardship ahead for the blissfully naked Adam and Eve. Melville will write about a man whose ugliness and wickedness he has painted in scrupulous strokes of degradation and suddenly turn aside to remark: "I never pitied any man more." Expulsion from the Garden, the hurt, pain, and willful malice he had observed in life, overwhelm the hope of reprieve by the martyrdom and Resurrection of Christ. In James Wood's imaginative reading, he is marked by the family Dutch Reform Calvinism to a greater degree than all are required to credit; but to find the Melvillean grip of metaphor hand in hand with the iron glove of Presbyterianism is paradoxically exhilarating.

The broad outlines of Melville's life are known to many who haven't read his books. Without the aggressive challenge of the books, he can have something of the shape of a woebegone fellow in a silent film. Every smile and bow is rewarded by a slap or a kick from a big, snaggletoothed, mustached philistine with a byline. How fitting it is that the penultimate scene will be a clerkship for nineteen years, from 1866 to 1885, in the waterfront Custom House. As a turn in a tale, the bureaucratic desk downtown is a dramatic fortuity. And then a mischievous addendum; as he lies stone-cold dead in the ground, a shower of gold coins clanks down on the tomb in the 1920s.

How did Melville, denied the sound of the gold coins of critical acclaim and all other aspects of his futurity, such as the endless listings under his name in the New York Public Library, view himself in the clerking years? There's a saturnine quality about him; he is capable of back-handed, cool acceptance of his destiny, pride in failure, which he capitalized as a kind of deity. He would not re-frain from his melancholy skepticism when book after book was rebuked for sacrilege; stubborn, gloomy fears for the drift of the nation did not move to a teatime cozi-ness for the pleasure of being in step.

The chronology of the Custom House period suggests, at least in the beginning years, a pathologically destructive resentment. The appointment began at the very end of 1866, and in the next few months Elizabeth Melville was seen by family and friends to be living in a nightmare. They sought to remove her from the house, to seek a legal separation, a drastic choice of action at the time. Melville was consumed by rage, breakdown, misery uncontrolled, given to violence in the household. He appeared to some to be insane. In the following months of this year, Mal-colm committed suicide, his act of separation.

The wife remained, and the husband persevered in his post for six days a week at a salary of four dollars a day, the calculation of dollar value at the time not lifting the wage above measliness. During his hours at work he was living with cannibals in woolen suits and ties and yet tat-tooed with ignorance and greed—some were arrested for embezzlement. In the midst of his fury Melville returned to his memory of the Holy Land, to the nighttime compo-sition of *Clarel,* with its length and its failure foreseen, an act of defiance, a scream for the scaffold.

Good families come into legacies; at least that would prove true when the Shaw cousins and aunts remembered the nice girl who had married a Melville. After nineteen years, three and a half weeks of service, a resignation from the Custom House came about. Son Stanwix died of tuberculosis far from home in San Francisco—another unhappy farewell in the male line. The difficult father, the raging river of print flowing downstream, managed to go on until 1891—the year he died at the age of seventy-two. The notice in the *New York Times* printed his name as Henry Melville. He was buried next to Malcolm in the Woodlawn Cemetery in the Bronx. He left behind a wife, two extant daughters and grandchildren; no illicit love affairs, no remaining love letters. His deepest attachments were to traveling, getting away, and writing, writing, writing, even during the late period that is known as Melville's *withdrawal.*

He died at home in his own house with a wife to care for him in his great distress and need. It appears he came to be grateful for her long years as Mrs. Melville, a calling certainly unexpected in her youth. Old age and habit, a settling down, a relief from the active "writhing" D. H. Lawrence named the condition of Herman Melville's soul. If so, this ornament and pride of our culture was to end his days with a sigh, a resigned, bearable, pedestrian loneliness.

AFTERWORD

THE BIBLIOGRAPHIC MATERIAL on Melville is intensive, extensive farming, ever piling up like threshed wheat to go off to the silo. Adding my own grain from a backyard plot is, perhaps, a presumption. Melville came into nineteenth-century American literature as a ground of miraculous opportunity. So little was known and so much to discover, to salvage from the heap, rake up the scraps lying about. Trunks of "stuff," letters and so on, will appear in a barn almost a century after his death. The yellowing, disintegrating pages are seized and carted away, as if by a scholarly sheriff. His library was around, and the little marks on the pages became a Rosetta stone to unravel the hieroglyphics of his thought. His range of reference will call for identification and commentary as lengthy as the work to which it is attached.

Melville's pages are the object of wild overinterpretation, even if it must be said that his genius is of such peculiarity, such insistence, discursiveness—or prolixity if the manner doesn't please—that it lends itself to flights of meaning. The poor whale is the father or the mother of us all, or is it God incarnated? Melville is a mystic or perhaps a brilliant nihilist out of Dostoevsky's *Possessed*. What was thought autobiography may turn out otherwise; on the other hand, a fact or two may establish autobiography once more. As for the Hereafter, does he voice a final Yea, or a No, in thunder?

This book is a reading of the work. Going through *Mardi, Pierre,* and the extremely long poem *Clarel* is a task, but inspired critics have found much of interest in the forbidding texts: thoughts on family and career in *Pierre,* on religion and Hawthorne in *Clarel.* I confess to having passed over them with abruptness. If a book can promote a reading of Melville, *Typee, Redburn,* certainly, and *The Confidence-Man,* possibly, can be added to the list of more or less *popular* titles such as *Moby-Dick* and the short fictions, "Benito Cereno," "Bartleby, the Scrivener," and *Billy Budd.*

In the matter of biography, I have given space to the obsessive relation with Hawthorne and to the "homo-erotic" refrain throughout the books. This recurrent musical theme has not done Melville's reputation any harm in the present landscape. I admit I have found it of interest and have marked the notes in the various places they are heard. What it means we cannot know. The fair young men have the dreamlike quality that fades at the break of day. And there we leave them.

BIBLIOGRAPHY

Melville Works

For the prose I have used *The Library of America*. 3 vols. 1982–84. Distributed by the Viking Press. Based on the text from the Northwestern-Newberry edition of *The Writings of Herman Melville*. Edited by Harrison Hayford, Hershel Parker, and G. Thomas Tanselle.

Collected Poems of Herman Melville. Edited by Howard P. Vincent. Hendricks House, 1947.

Selected Poems of Herman Melville. Edited by Hennig Cohen. Fordham University Press, 1991. Paperback edition.

Clarel. A Poem and Pilgrimage in the Holy Land. Edited by Harrison Hayford, Alma A. MacDougall, Hershel Parker, and G. Thomas Tanselle. Northwestern University Press and the Newberry Library, 1991. Paperback edition.

The Letters of Herman Melville. Edited by Merrell R. Davis and William H. Gilman. Yale University Press, 1960.

Journals. Edited by Howard C. Horsford and Lynn Horth. Northwestern University Press and the Newberry Library, 1989.

Biographies

Parker, Hershel. *Herman Melville*. A Biography. Vol. 1, 1819–51. Johns Hopkins University Press, 1996.

Bibliography

This most recent biography of Herman Melville, to be followed by a second volume on the remaining forty years, is 883 pages long. Mr. Parker is the leading Melville scholar, having written, edited, and annotated Melville material beyond measure. His is a prodigious enterprise, and it is hoped Mr. Parker will not say, as did George Eliot, that she began *Romola* as a young woman and finished it as an old one. Melville's life, after the few youthful years at sea, is perhaps known to most in the death and resurrection of his work; a dramatic pairing of which he knew only the first part. However, the Gansevoort and Melville families are rich in offspring; they write letters, take trips, work, marry and add new stock to the list, get into trouble. This horde of kinfolk gets more than its due in recent biographies. In addition, boats have captains and crews to be rooted out. For the ledger, there is money borrowed and spent. In the case of Herman Melville, the reviews of his books, because they tell you what he was going through, are more interesting than the doings of his relatives. In the maelstrom of facts, Hershel Parker's biography has swept through the Melville landscape and come up with just about everything under the sod. With a firm commitment and persistence, this biography is actually a pleasure to read. I have used it and used it and offer the all-knowing scholar my gratitude.

Robertson-Lorant, Laurie. *Melville, a Biography*. University of Massachusetts Press, 1996. Paperback edition.

A one-volume life, 620 pages. This biography appeared shortly before Mr. Parker's Volume 1. It is also industriously researched and a valuable, readable item indeed. She has the large family under her thumb—everything is here, picnics, headaches, housekeeping in the midst of the book after book written by the subject. Whenever possible, her tone is cheerful and intimate. I am grateful to the author for a book I turned to many times.

Books on Melville and Those Containing Chapters on His Work

All of the best critics and literary historians have written about Melville, and the brilliance of so many is a tribute to themselves and to the long-dead author they have studied with extraordinary vision and originality. This list is a bare, much-reduced citing of the treasures available.

Aaron, Daniel. *The Unwritten War: American Writers and the Civil War*. Alfred A. Knopf, 1973.

Arvin, Newton. *Herman Melville*. Viking Press, 1957. Paperback edition.

Chase, Richard. *Herman Melville: A Critical Study*. Macmillan, 1949.

————. *Melville: A Collection of Critical Essays*. Prentice-Hall, 1962.

Fiedler, Leslie. *Love and Death in the American Novel*. Dalkey Archive edition, 1997. Paperback edition.

Lawrence, D. H. *Studies in Classic American Literature*. Thomas Seltzer, 1923.

Matthiessen, F. O. *American Renaissance*. Oxford University Press, 1968. Paperback edition.

Oates, Joyce Carol. *Where I've Been and Where I'm Going*. A Plume Book. Published by the Penguin Group, 1999. Paperback edition.

Updike, John. *Hugging the Shore*. Alfred A. Knopf, 1983.

Wood, James. *The Broken Estate*. Random House, 1999.